Don Silver has written *A Parent's (and Grandparent's) Guide to Wills & Trusts* and the Internet futuristic column, *2020 Vision™*. He appears frequently in the media including the *NBC Network News and CNNfn*. *Baby Boomer Retirement* has been featured in *USA Weekend, Reuters, Knight-Ridder, Associated Press, America OnLine, 700 Club, Bottom Line Personal* and the *New York Daily News*.

PRAISE FOR
Baby Boomer Retirement

"Astute and provocative."
— RICHARD KAHLENBERG, "Earthwatch Column"
   LOS ANGELES TIMES

"Read this book and be the master of your own destiny."
— JAMES A. BARRY, Jr., CFP, Chairman of the Board of
   Barry Financial Group, Inc. and the host of
   JIM BARRY'S FINANCIAL SUCCESS, PBS

"*Baby Boomer Retirement* is a wake-up call to a generation that faces a precarious future without long-range financial planning. Don Silver has provided a crystal ball for peace of mind in your autumn years."
— LILLIAN VERNON, Founder and Chief Executive
   Officer, Lillian Vernon Corporation

"Don Silver's book offers sound advice to baby boomers who will benefit from the practical and emotional insights of *Baby Boomer Retirement*."
— GARY W. SMALL, M.D., Director, UCLA Center on
   Aging and co-author of *Parentcare*

more...

"Don Silver gives generous helpings of useful advice, not just for retirement but for right now, too."
— PAUL and SARAH EDWARDS, authors of
Working From Home

"How refreshing—a book that takes the complex and makes it understandable."
— KEVIN P. CONLEY, CLU, LUTCF
(and a baby boomer)

"A must-read recommendation for my baby boomer clients."
— ED LAPAZ, CPA

"A source of great ideas for readers of all generations."
— MARVIN S. FREEDMAN, Attorney-at-law

"A one-stop guide on the road to a secure, comfortable future. A must-read for anyone under age 65."
— MARILYN M. KRUSE, Investment Advisor
(and a baby boomer)

"Excellent ABC, nuts-and-bolts guide to a financially secure future."
— JAMES P. SOMERS, MBA, Financial Consultant
(and a baby boomer)

"The subtitle to *Baby Boomer Retirement* should really be 65 Wake-up Calls to Protect Your Future."
— LEON C. STERLING, Director, Sterling-Marc, Inc.
(and a baby boomer)

"A 'must-read' book for anyone with parents, children or plans to retire."
— MICHAEL SIEGEL, Esq.
(and a baby boomer)

more...

"*Baby Boomer Retirement* is a simple and direct road map to a secure future."
— ZEV YAROSLAVSKY, County Supervisor, County of Los Angeles

"This century has given us an unprecedented gift of long life. Looking ahead and saving for those new years of living is a must for all of us. If you want to enjoy your future, read this book."
— JAMES E. BIRREN, Associate Director, UCLA Center on Aging and co-author of *Where to Go From Here*

"Easy to read and informative."
— ROBERT GORDON, CPA

"The writing is clear and fresh. This book presents constructive advice on serious, complex issues."
— PATRICK RYAN, Fiscal Analyst (and a parent of a baby boomer)

"There is no better time for a book on retirement for late-blooming baby boomers who haven't spent enough time 'thinking about tomorrow.' This is a handy, easy-to-read guide to financial planning for people of every age."
— GLENDA WINDERS, syndicated columnist *COPLEY NEWS SERVICE*

"As a one-stop resource for busy boomers who want to take control of their financial lives and protect their children, their parents and their financial future, this guide to personal financial planning offers concrete advice on dealing with large mortgages, record-high college tuition, funding retirement plans for increased life spans and the need to care for aging parents."
— *ACCOUNTING TODAY*

more...

"Don Silver, once again, guides us safely through complicated financial territory with steps that are easily understood and applied toward financial success. This book is the ultimate gift for a baby boomer."
— CYNTHIA BOMAN THOMPSON, Certified Financial Planner (and a baby boomer)

"I am very impressed with the readability of this book."
— STANLEY R. HOFFMAN, Economist and Urban Planner

"*Baby Boomer Retirement* is a fun new book that's brimming with intelligence, good humor and solid advice on finances, healthy lifestyles and more."
— *POTENTIALS IN MARKETING*

"Retirement math starts with a piggy bank and ends with taking retirement distributions. One consideration affecting every homeowner's financial security is how quickly the mortgage is paid off. This book succinctly covers that as well as many other retirement issues."
— MICHAEL PELLECCHIA, Business Columnist *BOOKPAGE*

"*Baby Boomer Retirement* is the right book at the right time. It responds to this generation's heightened sensitivity to its imminent responsibility with intelligence, good humor and solid advice."
— *BUSINESS REVIEW*

more...

PRAISE FOR Don Silver's

A Parent's
(and Grandparent's)
Guide to Wills & Trusts

Jane Bryant Quinn put *A Parent's Guide to Wills & Trusts* by Don Silver on her holiday gift list in *Women's Day*.

"Excellent book...What also differentiates this book...is the writing itself. It is clear. It is concise. It is clever."
— *LOS ANGELES TIMES*

"This [book] is different: it's concisely written, uses simple language and features an easy-to-understand format."
— *CHICAGO SUN-TIMES*

"A practical, easily understood book that should be read by grandparents and parents alike."
— *GRANDPARENTING*
(a Universal Press Syndicate column)

"A *Parent's Guide* explains what parents and grandparents need to know about wills, trusts, taxes, special situations and health matters...In addition, Silver reveals seven myths about wills and trusts including the myth that joint tenancy is always the best way for parents and children to hold title to avoid probate."
— *SENIOR MAGAZINE*

more...

"Conversational and easy to understand, Silver uses wit, honesty and brevity (really!) to help parents figure out the best way to address problems."
— *SOUTH FLORIDA PARENTING*

"The book can serve as a tremendous tool for the layman...[Don Silver's] questions, answers and helpful hints are presented in a manner that makes the reader comfortable...a must...for [anyone] beginning the estate planning process."
— *LIFE ASSOCIATION NEWS*

"Easy-to-understand, no-nonsense approach to understanding wills and trusts...Unlike other estate planning books, *A Parent's Guide* combines real-life scenarios in a simple question and answer format."
— *FOCUS MAGAZINE*

"This book is excellent for the general public...well written, easy to read...great book for parents."
— *NATIONAL ALLIANCE FOR THE MENTALLY ILL ADVOCATE NEWSLETTER*

"This isn't just another probate/estate book. Tips on avoiding family disputes, considering tax impact and dealing with special circumstances, such as divorce, second marriages and special beneficiaries are remarkably specific and contain details no other general will book offers. *A Parent's Guide to Wills & Trusts* is *must* reading for all parents!"
— *WISCONSIN BOOKWATCH*

BABY Boomer Retirement

65 Simple Ways to
Protect Your Future

SECOND EDITION

BABY Boomer Retirement

65 Simple Ways to Protect Your Future

Don Silver

Adams-Hall Publishing
Los Angeles

Requests for such permissions should be addressed to:

Adams-Hall Publishing, PO Box 491002
Los Angeles, CA 90049-1002

No patent liability is assumed with respect to the use of the information contained
herein. While every precaution has been taken in the preparation of this book, the
publisher and the author assume no responsibility for errors or omissions. Neither is
any liability assumed for damages resulting from the use of the information contained
herein.

Assume that all products, company names and Web sites listed in the index and the
book are trademarks and/or registered trademarks.

Library of Congress Cataloging-in-Publication Data

Silver, Don
Baby Boomer Retirement: 65 Simple Ways to Protect Your Future (2nd edition)
        p.   cm.
    Includes index.
    ISBN 0-944708-49-8
1. Retirement income—United States—Planning. 2. Retirees—United States—Finance,
Personal. 3. Baby boom generation—United States. I. Title.
HG179.S474 1998
332.024'01—dc 21   97-42271
                                                                       CIP

Cover Design by Hespenheide Design (805/373-7336)

Adams-Hall books are available at special, quantity discounts for bulk purchases for
sales promotions, premiums, fund-raising or educational use. For details, contact:
Special Sales Director, Adams-Hall Publishing, PO Box 491002, Los Angeles, CA
90049-1002 (1/800-888-4452 or 310/826-1851).

Printed in the United States of America
20 19 18 17 16 15 14 13 12 11 10 9 8 7 6 5 4 3 2 1
First printing 1998

Acknowledgments

Although writing a book is a very personal process, every author needs the help of others to produce the best result.

I want to first express my thanks to those individuals who took time out of their very busy schedules to review the advance proof and offer praiseworthy comments. My deepest appreciation goes to James A. Barry, Jr., James E. Birren, Kevin P. Conley, Paul and Sarah Edwards, Marvin S. Freedman, Robert Gordon, Stanley R. Hoffman, Richard Kahlenberg, Marilyn M. Kruse, Ed Lapaz, Patrick Ryan, Michael Siegel, Gary W. Small, James P. Somers, Leon C. Sterling, Cynthia Boman Thompson, Lillian Vernon and Zev Yaroslavsky.

Special thanks go to Phyllis Billings, Michael Siegel and James P. Somers for their helpful editorial suggestions and comments and to Gary Hespenheide of Hespenheide Design for another wonderful cover.

Writing a book often entails sacrifice on the part of the author balanced by support from the author's family. A special thank you to Emily, Marilyn, and Ralph for their loving support. To my young son, Charlie, let me say that Daddy looks forward to spending even more time with you now that the book is completed. And, I'm very proud that you have told me you're starting to save for retirement now that you're six years old. Finally, I have been blessed with a loving and caring wife, Susan, who is also my best friend. I could not have written this book without her support.

Don Silver

Disclaimer

All of the names and situations in this book are hypothetical and the resemblance to anyone's actual situation is purely coincidental.

This book is intended to provide accurate information. It is not intended, however, to render any legal, tax, accounting, financial, or other professional advice or services. You should therefore use this book as a general guide only. In addition, this book contains information that was available only up to the time of printing.

Although there are certain steps described in this book that you can take yourself, this book is not intended to be a substitute for the professional assistance of an attorney, accountant, financial planner, and life insurance agent.

Laws do change with some frequency. That's why you must discuss your situation with qualified professionals before relying solely on the information you may find here or anywhere else.

Contents

Introduction   1

BUILDING YOUR NEST EGG

1. The big change in retirement planning: you might
   want to avoid traditional IRAs   9
2. Preventing Social InSecurity   11
3. Honey, they shrunk the pension!   15
4. Building a nest egg from scratch, starting with
   the power of a piggy bank   19
5. Don't say no to free money   20
6. A penny saved is not a penny earned   21
7. The secret way to save for retirement   23
8. Avoiding a dozen common errors   27
9. How to select a financial advisor   31
10. When to start building your nest egg   34
11. The benefit of a good foundation   36
12. Learning new retirement math: how to
    calculate the right-size nest egg   39
13. Eight ways to make sure your retirement
    investments are right for you   46
14. 401(k) plan do's and don'ts   49
15. The federally insured surprise: retirement assets
    in banks may not be fully federally insured   52
16. The new IRA game   53
17. Eight ways to reduce your income taxes   56
18. Saving taxes on distributions from retirement plans   61
19. Living long and in comfort: look to annuities   63
20. How to take years off your mortgage payments   69
21. Houses and the 1997 tax act in a nutshell   73
22. Big brother taking care of his own: 403(b)
    and 457 plans   75
23. See the USA with an MSA   76

IMPROVING THE QUALITY OF YOUR LIFE

24. Adding value to your life 79
25. Simplifying your life 81
26. Larger houses and improving the quality of life
 for the sandwich generation 84
27. Becoming a stay-at-home parent can pay off big 86
28. A working retirement 90
29. Life insurance that pays while you're alive and ill 91
30. Who do you trust—with your money and your life? 92
31. Protecting your privacy 95

MAKING THE KIDS AND STEP-KIDS WEALTHY AND WISE

32. The right and wrong ways to save for your
 children's college education 99
33. Calculating a college-size nest egg 112
34. Keeping Uncle Sam out of your estate 116

TYING OR RETYING THE KNOT

35. What you must know before you marry or remarry 123
36. Will Uncle Sam tear up part of your marital
 agreement? 125
37. Filling out college aid applications before and
 after the wedding 126
38. For better or for worse—what can that *really* mean? 127
39. Protecting the inheritance for your kids 128

MORE WAYS TO PROTECT THE NEST EGG

40. Refinancing for the better 133
41. Protecting retirement plan assets 134
42. Life insurance do's and don'ts 135
43. How to plan for rainy days: umbrella insurance 136
44. Avoiding probate with a living trust 137

Contents

MOVING TO GREENER PASTURES

45. Finding the right place for your parents to retire   141
46. Six questions you need to ask before moving
     to a new state or staying right where you are   143
47. Paying all cash for your home for retirement
     may not be wise   146

NURSING HOME NEWS

48. What your parents should be doing now to avoid
     going broke paying future nursing home costs   149
49. New nursing home insurance program may give
     special protection to your parents' assets   155

LOOKING OUT FOR YOUR PARENTS

50. Telling your parents the financial facts of life
     before they remarry   159
51. Making sure your parents' health coverage doesn't
     expire at the border   161
52. The joint tenancy surprise: the down side of
     holding title as joint tenants   162
53. The income tax surprise all siblings need to know   165
54. The death tax surprise all siblings need to know   166
55. Mentioning the unmentionable   167

INSURING YOUR RETIREMENT

56. The three questions you should ask about life
     insurance—before you buy   171
57. Buying the right amount and kind of life insurance   173
58. Ways to avoid death tax on life insurance   180
59. The right and wrong way to name beneficiaries   181
60. What to look for in a disability insurance policy   183

TAKING CARE OF BUSINESS

61. Three steps every business owner has to consider   187
62. What you need to know if you have a partner
     in real estate or business   189

MAKING MONEY FROM YOUR PAPERWORK

63. How financial records can save you taxes
     on your house   193
64. How financial records can save you taxes
     on stocks and mutual funds   195
65. Finding lost treasures   197

Appendix

Examples of Social Security retirement, disability and
survivors benefits   201

Great Way to Search the Internet   203

Software and Internet Sites of interest   204

Books Worth Considering   206

Index

    207

Introduction

Retirement planning for baby boomers is unique and particularly challenging because the biological and financial clocks are ticking away in changing economic times. Quite simply, there are going to be two groups of baby boomers at retirement age—those who prepared and those who should have. This book will help you prepare for your retirement years—while there's still time.

And the time is fast approaching. Every day 10,000 baby boomers are turning age 40 and another 10,000 are celebrating their 50th birthday. That means every year another four million of us baby boomers are reaching the Big "FOUR OH" and the same number are attaining age fifty.

Retirement planning for baby boomers is unique due to the unprecedented lifespan of boomers and the transformation of the traditional sources for retirement income including Social Security and company pension plans.

At no other time in history has a group had to confront and plan for a retirement that might last as long as 30 or 40 years. The 77 million baby boomers should feel fortunate. At the turn of the century, the average American could look forward to a life span of just 47 years.

On the other hand, this longevity may force many baby boomers to continue working during "retirement," especially if the retirement years include the challenge of paying for the college education of a child or children and supporting aging parents.

Unless we develop goals and a plan for the future and learn how to deal with the never-ending changes in the economy and our society, we will be unprepared to meet the challenges of the 21st century.

Just as we have seen how savings and loan institutions could fall apart, the same may happen even to Social Security. A bi-partisan panel in Congress has warned that Social Security benefits may not be there just when baby boomers will be ready to draw on them. Back in 1945, there were 42 workers paying in for every beneficiary drawing Social Security bene-fits. By the time the last boomers reach age 65, the ratio will be only two workers for each beneficiary.

A FUTURISTIC FANTASY: KEEPING UP WITH THE JONES FAMILY IN THE 21st CENTURY

When the year 2020 rolls around, most boomers will look back 20 years to the year 2000 and say "I wish I knew financially then what I know now."

In the year 2020, over 30 million of the 77 million baby boomers born between 1946 and 1964 will be at least age 65. That number will grow by more than three million per year until the year 2029.

Boomers who were depending upon Social Security for their sole or main support will be disappointed. However, those boomers who started saving on their own around the end of the 20th Century will be able to keep up with Joneses down the block.

What most boomers won't remember is back in 1998, there were three workers per Social Security beneficiary. In 2020, there will only be about two workers per beneficiary. Oh sure, Social Security will have survived but only with sacrifices: a later retirement age, reduced benefits, increased taxation of the reduced benefits and increased payroll taxes for Generations X and Y, the generations that follow the baby boomers.

2

Introduction

In 2020, millions of baby boomers will want their Social Security retirement benefits to start. Some will have to wait longer than they thought. By the year 2020, the retirement age will be at least age 70 and probably age 72 (even under the law in 1997, "normal retirement age" for baby boomers under the Social Security system is not age 65—it's between 66 and 67 depending upon one's date of birth).

If Social Security isn't totally there and boomers haven't saved enough on their own or through work retirement plans, there may be an asset of last resort to fund retirement—their houses.

Untold millions of baby boomers will seek to sell their houses to fund their retirement. Due to the 1997 tax law change, many boomers will have stopped keeping track of house improvements thinking that there could never be more than $500,000 in profits from a sale of their house. (According to the 1997 tax act, married boomers can exempt up to $500,000 in gains from federal income tax with single boomers exempting half that amount.) What they did not know was that the "Great Inflation of 2010" added a zero to the selling price of every house but the tax laws were not revised to reflect the change in the marketplace. After all, with the government so short of revenue, why not tax every available source?

With housing so expensive and the best prospective buyers, the Generation Xers, strapped to pay the high income and payroll tax rates on inflation-boosted incomes to meet the incredible cost to fund "Minicare" (the new name for the stripped down Medicare program) and "Social InSecurity" (as it will be known), houses won't sell like hotcakes. Even hotcakes won't be selling like hotcakes in restaurants because the high cost of living will prevent most people from eating out like they used to do in the 1990s.

As a result, many families will have up to four generations living together to save money. Children will get to know and be taken care of by their baby boomer grandparents and their great-grandparents. As these 65-year-old baby boomers age with their 85- and 90-year-old parents, they will all have much more in common than they did in the 1960s.

Due to financial necessity, the sheer force of numbers and their continuing trend-setting ability, baby boomers will continue to work productively during the "silver years" (the golden years won't start until you're at least age 80). The latest national phrase will be "Don't trust anyone under 65!"

But some things won't change. Boomers will still be looking down the street, still trying to keep up with the Jones family, who started saving for a rainy day back in the good old days, the 1990s.

HOW TO PREVENT THE 2020 FANTASY AND CHANGE THE OUTCOME FOR YOU

Up to now, there have been three pillars of retirement planning. One of them, Social Security, needs an overhaul to be viable. The second pillar, company pension plan benefits, is being reduced or eliminated as part of the corporate down-sizing and cost-cutting trend.

What's left is the third pillar of retirement planning—personal savings and investments. In the past, personal savings and investments were seen as a way of merely enhancing an already secure retirement. For baby boomers they may be the most important component of our retirement planning. Time is on the side of baby boomers, but not for long. Building up sufficient personal savings and investments for retirement will require a major shift in thinking. "Saving" may become the mantra of our generation.

This book is designed to make the process of planning for your retirement easier by guiding you through the three pillars of retirement planning as well as the interconnected legal, health-related, family, lifestyle and personal issues you will need to address for yourself, your spouse, your children, and your parents. As an attorney with over 20-years experience in estate planning, a fellow baby boomer and the author of books on baby boomer retirement and estate planning, I'll cover these issues as well as the "financial time bombs" you may face now or in the 21st century.

The bottom line is that it's essential to start planning now. Planning can save you money, stress and aggravation. Also, some opportunities will only be available if you've anticipated and mapped out a strategy in advance to deal with them. On the financial side alone, if you delay retirement planning by even 10 years, it may cost you three times as much each month to accumulate the same nest egg.

The goal of this book is to provide you with a clear understanding of the key issues so you can take the right steps now to protect your future and that of your loved ones.

BUILDING YOUR NEST EGG

1.

The big change in retirement planning: you might want to avoid traditional IRAs

With the passage of the Taxpayer Relief Act of 1997, the rules for retirement planning have changed.

Now, there is a big tax incentive to keep at least some of your assets *out* of traditional individual retirement accounts (IRAs) and retirement plans in some cases. The tax act also introduced a new kind of IRA, the Roth IRA.

When you invest in the traditional IRA, you may get a current income tax deduction for your contribution. However, when you take the assets out, you are taxed for income tax purposes at the ordinary income tax rates. Ordinary income tax rates are from 15% to 39.6% on the federal level depending upon your income. State income tax is on top of this federal income tax. Distributions from retirement plans are subject to the same income tax bite, too. By contrast, the 1997 tax act gives two ways to cut the ultimate tax bill.

First, starting in 1998, you can invest in a Roth IRA. With this IRA, you don't receive an income tax deduction for the contribution. You are using after-tax money to fund the contribution. However, the payback can be big. If all of the Roth IRA requirements are met, then all of the growth and withdrawals are *income-tax free*. Since the Roth IRA requirements may change over time as to who is eligible to make a contribution and how long your money must be kept in the IRA, you should always check with your tax advisor before making a contribution or a withdrawal. With a Roth IRA, you

Benefits could be hundreds of thousands of dollars

Most people underestimate the potential size of these benefits. The benefits could be worth hundreds of thousands of dollars to you and your loved ones.

For example, if a husband or wife passed away in 1997, leaving a surviving spouse and two young children (ages four and two), and earnings of the deceased spouse were at the maximum Social Security levels, the surviving family currently could receive up to $30,000 per year for many years. Over the years, the family benefits could amount to hundreds of thousands of dollars. (To see typical retirement, disability and survivor benefits, take a look at the tables on pages 201-202 in the Appendix.)

To avoid being shortchanged, you need to make sure Social Security has recorded your earnings correctly since it is *earnings* that determine the benefit amounts for you and your family members.

When you or your family members apply for any of these possible Social Security benefits, how will you or they know if the benefits are based on the correct amount of your earnings? There is a simple way to find out and it costs one stamp every three years.

Form SSA-7004

To keep an eye on the information being used by Social Security, you need to complete a *Request for Earnings and Benefit Estimate Statement* (Form SSA-7004) at least every three years.

The form is free and it's easy to obtain (call 1/800-772-1213 to order the form). Then you just fill out the simple form and mail it to the Social Security Administration.

Social Security will mail a listing of your earnings (according to their records) and a projection of your Social Security retirement, disability and survivors benefits. You just need to compare one or two lines of your income tax returns with the benefit statement to determine whether the Social Security records are accurate. If there is any mistake in their records, you should have it corrected before it's too late.

How you can be shortchanged

Social Security has to deal with the earnings of every working person in the country every year. Do you think it's possible when keying in information for more than 130 million workers that a data entry operator ever leaves off a digit (changing $31,000 to $3,100) or reverses digits (changing $31,000 to $13,000)? It just may be your luck that you'll be the one this happens to. Even if Social Security never makes a mistake, could your company make one in sending in your earnings record?

The name is the game

Have you always filled in your payroll forms exactly the same way or have you sometimes used a full middle name and other times just an initial? The safest way is to always match the name on your Social Security card identically to that on employment forms, including W-2 forms.

And, if you're a woman who has married and/or divorced and changed her name, have you advised Social Security of all name changes?

No problem, you say, since when the time rolls around to collect benefits, you'll double check everything. That's what you say. There are two problems with this reasoning.

First, in the year 2020 you probably won't be able to *find* your tax returns to verify your earnings from the 1990s. Secondly, and more important, even if you could locate those records, it could be too late under the law to make Social Security correct its records. The law makes it your responsibility to be sure Social Security records your earnings correctly. There are time limits for correcting errors. You may lose tremendous benefits for the rest of your life (and reduce your family's benefits, too) if a mistake is reported too late.

How long do you have to report a mistake?

In general, you have three years, three months, and 15 days after the year in which the earnings were earned or wages paid to report a needed correction. To correct 1997 earnings, you would need to notify Social Security no later than April 15, 2001. It might be possible to extend the correction period.

In 1999, Social Security is scheduled to automatically send statements to all workers age 25 and over. However, don't wait or depend on this to happen since you may lose the chance to correct earnings (and thus benefits) attributable to earlier periods. All it takes now is one phone call, buying a stamp and spending a few minutes to protect the future of you and your family members.

On-line information

Go to the Social Security Website (http://www.ssa.gov) and look up a wealth of information including explanations, publications and examples.

3.

Honey, they shrunk the pension!

Besides possible miscalculations in Social Security benefits just discussed on pages 11 to 14, don't overlook the possibility of mistakes occurring in your company's retirement plan (or your own plan if you are self-employed). Even small errors can grow to significant dollar losses for you since the effects will compound over the years.

Again, as the years go by, how will you be able to find and correct a mistake made in the prior century? The answer is, you won't, so monitor your plan each year.

Some surprises are turning up in retirement plans

Just when retirement plans are growing in size and importance, some surprises are turning up in retirement plan distributions.

There are many types of retirement plans including 401(k) and defined benefit plans. With 401(k) plans, employees provide the bulk of the funding and the final size of the nest egg isn't known until retirement. With defined benefit plans, it's the employer who provides the funding and the retirement benefit is a fixed percentage of an employee's earnings (usually reduced by the amount of expected Social Security benefits).

Although defined benefit plans are generally being phased out over time and replaced by 401(k) plans, there are millions of Americans currently receiving benefits from defined benefit plans. These plans have been the focus of an audit by the government's Pension Benefit Guaranty Corporation ("PBGC").

The PBGC's latest audit discovered that more than 13% of defined benefit pension participants were being underpaid. It appears at this time that the underpayments were unintentional. Most mistakes have resulted from one or more of the following factors: defective software, errors in inputting earnings, length of employment and life expectancies as well as just the complexity of pension laws.

Some of these mistakes could have been prevented if employees double-checked their employer's records each year. However, in many cases, it takes a pension expert playing detective to uncover the shortages. It may be worth it for you to call the National Center for Retirement Benefits, Inc. ("NCRB"). The NCRB pays for all of the expenses of investigation and it receives a fee only from the benefits recovered for you. The NCRB does not handle governmental or union/multi-employer plans. If you call the NCRB (1/800/666-1000), you can receive a free brochure and a list of 30 serious errors and problems found in pension and profit sharing plans.

Steps to take now

Don't wait for Congress to reform the retirement plan laws before taking the following steps:

• First, get a Summary Plan Description ("SPD") from your employer that tells you how retirement benefits are calculated and paid out. Read the description and ask questions until you really understand it.

• Before changing jobs and giving up your current retirement plan benefits, look at the new company's SPD to see what's in store for you. In general, if you're covered by an old-style defined benefit plan with one employer for your entire career as compared to having such a plan with four different employers, your ultimate pension may be twice as large.

• When reviewing the SPD (and annual statements from your employer), look to see:

(1) whether retirement plan benefits are determined just from your base salary or whether bonuses, overtime and commissions are also included;

(2) whether your employer will match all, part, or none of the contributions made by you to the company's 401(k) plan;

(3) what the limit is for contributions by you to the company plan;

(4) whether employer contributions each year are based on a percentage of your salary that year or determined by a formula that also considers your age and the number of years you have until retirement;

(5) whether retirement benefits (in the case of certain pension plans) are based on just your highest-earning years (no matter when they occurred in your employment career);

(6) whether your time worked at companies co-owned or part of the same family of companies is counted;

(7) how years of service are calculated if you take a pregnancy break or some other leave of absence (or even another job) and then come back (see page 62 too); and

(8) whether your pension is reduced by a portion or all of your Social Security retirement benefit (this is commonly called "Social Security integration").

• Write every employer you've worked for to see if you can find any forgotten retirement and/or life insurance benefits waiting for you or your heirs.

• Call or write your Senators and Congressional representative and ask them to simplify the pension laws to help eliminate underpayments.

It could be a long wait until you receive your pension benefits

It's not bad enough that you might be shortchanged on your retirement benefits. It could be worse. You could have to wait decades for the underpayments to begin.

Imagine, that you left your employer when you were age 35. You're sitting by the mailbox waiting for the payout of your retirement plan benefits so you can pay the bills until you find your next job. You may have a long wait.

In many cases, employers can legally wait until you reach age 65 to distribute your retirement benefits. It doesn't matter that you need your vested benefits paid to you in 30 days, not 30 years. Again, take a look at your plan's Summary Plan Description to see what your employer is required to do on distributions. The good news is that many employers make lump-sum distributions in a matter of months, not years.

Before a retirement plan distribution is made, it's always a good idea to first get tax advice as to the income tax consequences of the different distribution choices and how to handle loans taken against your retirement benefits.

For many of us, our employer's retirement plan may be more important in the long-run than Social Security benefits. Be vigilant and take the time to become educated. When you receive your employer's retirement plan statement each year, double check it. Surprises can be fun but not usually with retirement distributions.

4.

Building a nest egg from scratch, starting with the power of a piggy bank

There's a simple way you can start saving now even if you have enormous mortgage, personal and education costs. Don't overlook the power of a piggy bank as a way to start a retirement and education savings plan. There's an estimated eight billion dollars in change lying around the house across the United States.

It's painless to take your change each day and put it in a piggy bank or even a jar. Whether you earmark these coins for your children's college education or your own retirement (see No. 32 on pages 99 through 111 for the pros and cons of each approach), it's a simple step well worth taking.

The following example illustrates the financial power of piggy banks. Assume, starting at age 35, each evening you put that day's loose change in a piggy bank. If, on the average, you feed piggy 50¢ a day and also throw in an extra dollar every month, at the end of every three months, you'd have around $50 to invest. You could put this money in a Roth IRA or other retirement plan that would grow tax free or, at least, tax-deferred until distributions were taken out (subject to certain restrictions, of course).

If your contributions average a 10% yearly return (which is the average growth for stocks since 1926), then at age 70, you'd have a retirement fund from your piggy bank of around $33,000. If every day you also add a dollar bill, you'd have around $100,000 in hand at age 70. Nice piggy.

5.

Don't say no to free money

Of all the types of retirement plans at work, the most common one is the 401(k). With 401(k) plans, employees provide the bulk of the funding. However, most employers match some or all of the employee contribution.

If your company has one of those "matching" 401(k) plans and you're not participating at all or not participating to the fullest extent possible, you're giving up free money. Over the long-haul, you could be passing up tens or hundreds of thousands of dollars including the growth of employer contributions.

If you're highly paid and you have your employer withhold the maximum amount from each paycheck, you may be getting shortchanged on your employer's matching contribution. The reason is that your 401(k) contribution limitation may be reached too early, say in October instead of December, by making the maximum contribution from each paycheck. If you reach the maximum contribution amount too early in the year, that shuts off your employer's matching contribution for the rest of the year. Instead, you should reach the maximum contribution more gradually by making a lower percentage contribution from your paycheck. Talk to the plan administrator at work to set up the right schedule for your level of income.

The best way to think of this is that in a long-distance race, you don't want to run too fast or else you won't be able to finish the race with a kick at the end.

6.

A penny saved is not a penny earned

Ben Franklin was only half right when he said "A penny saved is a penny earned." He didn't have to deal with income tax. I wonder what the Boston Tea Party would have been like today if our Founding Fathers had to fill out today's income tax returns.

These days, if you earn two additional dollars on top of your regular income, you have about one dollar left after federal and state income tax and Social Security and Medicare taxes.

Prioritize your money

You need to prioritize your monthly investments between retirement planning, educational expenses and high-interest, non-deductible debt. Your best investment may be to pay off debt first since you may not find an investment that pays as much as your debt costs you. And the bonus to this strategy is that less debt means less stress.

The best way to learn how to prioritize your money is to carry around a small notebook for one month and write down every single penny you spend. You'll be amazed at where your money goes and how you'll discover painless ways to save money each day.

The "36% return" on your investment

You may have debt on which interest is not deductible (such as personal credit card interest). If you are paying 18% interest on unpaid balances, do you need to earn 36% on your investments or earn the equivalent wages to wind up with the money to pay the 18% interest? It will depend on your income tax bracket. The bottom line is no matter what income tax bracket you are in, you are paying off credit card interest with after-tax, non-deductible dollars.

You may also want to shop around for another credit card with a lower interest rate. Before you switch, make sure you understand whether the lower rate is only for a limited time period. If so, you might get stuck with a much higher rate after the introductory lower rate period. Also, if you are counting on the lower rate applying to prior charges that are being transferred over to a new card, make sure that this indeed is the case. Otherwise, the new rate may only apply to new charges. Pay as much as you can each month to reduce the amount owed as well as the accompanying tension.

It may be wiser to take out a home equity loan to pay off credit card debts so the interest portion of your payments qualifies for an income tax deduction (check with your tax advisor since not all home equity loans qualify for this deduction).

Before seeing a home equity loan as a cure-all, remember, that if you default on a home equity loan, you may lose your house.

You may also want to consider refinancing the loan on your house to lower your monthly payments. Before taking this step, make sure that you consider (1) the costs vs. the benefits especially if you'll want or have to sell your house within a few years of the refinancing and (2) whether you are adding additional years for the payback of your loan. Also see No. 40 on page 133 and No. 47 on page 146.

Remember, saving money is a great way to make money! It beats working for it.

7.

The secret way to save for retirement

The secret way to save for retirement is *not* to budget for it. If you try to budget a share for retirement savings, this item will always be at the bottom of the list since all other expenditures either have a more immediate, short-term benefit or may (inevitably) prove to be more urgent. Instead, you need to make the saving process so automatic that it doesn't require a conscious decision or act by you.

Automatic withdrawals from your paycheck or your checking account that go directly to an IRA, other retirement plan account or into personal savings and investments can achieve this result. And with some retirement plans, there can be an added benefit of your contributions saving you income tax each year, too.

The sooner you set up an *automatic savings plan*, the more you'll have at retirement. A simple example shows the benefit of starting to save for retirement today.

Scenario One

At age 30, you put $2,000 into an IRA or other *tax-deferred* retirement plan (i.e., one that grows income-tax free until distributions are taken out). At ages 31 and 32, you also add $2,000 each year. Then, you stop making any contributions. If those three $2,000 contributions generate a return of 10% per year, then at age 65 you will have $140,000.

That's $140,000 from three $2,000 contributions.

Scenario Two

If, instead, you waited until age 45 to make your first $2,000 contribution and then you made $2,000 contributions religiously every year for the next 19 years under the same conditions as Scenario One, you would have only $114,000 at age 65.

Compound interest/compound growth

How can 20 contributions of $2,000 produce less than three contributions of $2,000? The answer is *compound interest* (also sometimes called *compound growth*).

Compound interest or compound growth refers to the effect over time of an investment growing in value *and* the reinvested growth also increasing over time. With a savings account, compound interest lets you receive interest on your interest. The longer you've invested, the greater the opportunity for compound interest or growth.

Compound interest is the reason why the earlier you start saving for retirement or your children's college education, the less you'll have to put away each month. With compound interest, once you've worked for your money, your money starts working for you.

Tax-deferred and tax-free investments

There is a second component to successfully saving for retirement. If you use *tax-deferred investments* (e.g., traditional IRAs, retirement plans and certain other investments) or tax-free investments (e.g., Roth IRAs - see pages 53-55) to save for retirement, you'll achieve your goal sooner.

A tax-deferred investment is one that isn't reduced by income tax while it is growing (income tax is paid later when distributions are taken out). It's no mystery why a tax-deferred investment grows faster than a non-deferred one. If the IRS suddenly announced you didn't have to pay income tax, your paycheck or profit would go up and you would have more money.

When you pay income tax on increases in your investments during the growing years of a *non*-tax-deferred investment, it's like a baseball team with one or more of its players on the bench—you probably won't be able to cover all the bases.

The 1997 tax act introduced a new kind of savings vehicle, the Roth IRA. With a Roth IRA, the tax benefit comes at the end. Withdrawals (including the contributions and the growth over the years) may be income tax free. The contributions are not tax-deductible. The Roth IRA may not just defer (delay) income tax. If all the requirements are met, the Roth IRA can be federal income tax free.

With a traditional IRA, it's the reverse. The contributions may be tax-deductible up front but everything is subject to income tax when it is paid out.

What's better for you? It depends upon your particular circumstances now and at the time you retire. If the requirements are met, a traditional IRA can be converted into a Roth IRA. There will be income tax paid at the time of the conversion (which if done in 1998 can be spread out over four years) but not at the time of distribution if all the requirements are satisfied.

The first step is to see if your income level permits you to contribute to a traditional and/or Roth IRA. Those numbers will change over time so you need to talk to your accountant each year.

The next step is to see what federal and state income tax brackets you are in now to see how much you'll benefit from a current income tax deduction for a traditional IRA contribution. Then, you need to project your income level at retirement to estimate what bracket you'll be in at the time you begin to withdraw your IRA money.

Then, go through the same analysis on the Roth IRA with your accountant.

Finally, run the numbers on investing in your personal name outside of any kind of IRA to see if the long-term capital gains rules produce an even better income tax result for you and your family and more flexibility for using the money at any time (before and after retirement).

Ideally, you should arrange for automatic monthly payments to come off the top and go into some form of investment, inside or outside of an IRA or retirement plan. If that isn't possible due to ever increasing financial demands, then whenever you get a bonus, raise or refund, why not take all or a portion of that windfall to open up or add to your savings or retirement fund?

So what's the lesson? Invest as much as you can, as early as you can, to have the greatest opportunity for tax-deferred or tax-free compound growth or long-term capital gains taxation. If you delay, you will pay!

8.

Avoiding a dozen common errors

You may prevent a dozen mistakes that frequently occur in retirement planning by taking the following steps:

1. Maximize contributions to *tax-deferred* retirement plans where your employer matches at least part of your contribution (see page 20).

2. Diversify investments (don't put all of your nest eggs in the same basket).

3. Consider the effects of inflation (see page 41).

4. Assess your risk comfort level.

5. Avoid a risky investment that promises too big a profit—if an investment sounds too good to be true, listen to your intuition.

6. Select your financial advisor very carefully.

7. Take the time and effort to monitor how your investments are doing (even if you have a financial advisor).

8. Start saving for retirement as soon as possible.

9. Retire later rather than earlier—a couple of extra years sometimes boosts checks by 25% or more, may avoid early retirement withdrawal penalties and delays dipping into the retirement nest egg.

10. Get professional advice before withdrawing your retirement assets when you leave your job. In some cases, such as with company stock in a retirement plan, you may save tremendous income tax in the long run for you and your heirs by *not* rolling over the stock into an IRA and, instead, putting it into your individual name. Although there will be some income tax due right away by doing this, have your accountant run the numbers to see how beneficial this technique might be in your case (and also explain how capital gains tax and the "step-up in basis" rule could apply to reduce income taxes for you and your family).

11. Calculate the effects of income taxes, including taxes due on early withdrawals of investments. Try to stay aware of new pension, income tax and estate tax laws. Some examples are discussed below.

Pension laws

Congress may soon approve a new kind of pension plan to allow more pension funds to move from job to job, have 100% vesting (no forfeitures) and permit boomers to make extra contributions to catch up for not saving enough in prior years.

Income tax laws

Mutual funds pay out almost of all of their income each year to the holders of the funds. Mutual funds are companies with professional managers that pool your money with that of other investors to buy stocks and/or bonds.

Some funds have larger gains than others that will have to come out sometime (and be taxable to you even if you haven't sold the fund). Since that's taxable income to the fundholder (you) including interest, dividends and short and long-term capital gains, find out before you invest in a fund how much pent-up profit trouble could come bursting into your bubble even if the growth occurred before you became involved with the fund. Even if this income is automatically reinvested for you in the fund, it's taxable income for the fundholder (you) that year unless the mutual fund is in a tax-deferred plan such as a traditional IRA (or a potentially tax-free Roth IRA). The bottom line is that you may need to shell out big bucks in income tax for gains you are reinvesting and not putting into your pocket that year.

If you tend to buy and hold stocks and mutual funds for a long period of time, you might want these investments held in your personal name, rather than in an IRA or other retirement plan. This could entitle you to favorable federal long-term capital gains income tax (a federal income tax of 8% to 20% on the gain) as compared to the traditional IRA/retirement plan distribution income tax (up to a federal "ordinary" income tax of 39.6%). Some retirement plan distributions qualify for special income-tax averaging rates. Ask your accountant about the best way for you to receive distributions.

Likewise, you'll want to consider having mutual funds owned in your personal name that generate more long-term capital gains tax as compared to ordinary income tax. Be sure to ask how "tax efficient" a mutual fund is and its rate of turnover (how quickly a fund sells its investments to determine how much you'll owe each year in long-term capital gains tax or ordinary income tax on assets held in your personal name). Stay on top of this issue because the turnover rate in the past may not be the turnover rate in the future.

If there is a lot of change in your investments, you might want to hold assets inside a 401(k), IRA or other retirement plan since no income tax is paid until distributions are made. And, with a Roth IRA, there may not be any income tax due (see pages 53-55).

The rule of thumb is to have high turnover rates in tax-deferred and tax-free accounts and low turnover rates in your individual name accounts.

Estate tax laws

The Taxpayer Relief Act of 1997 increased the amount that may be left free of death tax. Be sure to have your will and/or trust reviewed to see that you are utilizing the new law to the best advantage for your estate.

12. Consider non-tax costs of investments (e.g., high fees if you want to bail out early from an annuity; lack of liquidity so that it's difficult to get your money out of a limited partnership; or high annual management costs with some mutual funds).

9.

How to select a financial advisor

Will you spend more time thinking about the topping for your next pizza than you will in selecting a financial advisor?

Among the questions you should *ask yourself* are:

1. Does my accountant know and recommend a good financial advisor?

2. Do I know other clients who have worked with the advisor for at least several years?

   Ideally, you would answer "yes" to both of these questions but a "yes" to either one may be sufficient.

3. Have I called the state regulatory agency to see if there are any disciplinary actions against the advisor?

Among the questions you should *ask the prospective advisor* are:

1. Am I like your typical client?

2. What are your qualifications and length of experience?

3. How will you be compensated? Will you earn a fee *(a)* on commissions for selling investments, *(b)* a fee for services but no commissions, or *(c)* a combination of a fee and commissions? Is your fee a flat fee including all services or is it calculated on an hourly basis at a specified hourly rate?

All things being equal, the fee with no commission, option *(b)*, should result in the most objective advice for you.

4. Will you let me see financial plans of other clients like me with the client names blocked out?

The *prospective financial advisor should ask you (and you should be prepared to answer)* at least the following questions:

1. What are your financial and personal goals, short-term and long-term?

2. How much risk are you willing to take on investments?

3. What are your needs for cash besides what is invested in long-term investments?

The *financial advisor should do* at least the following:

1. Fully explain, orally and in writing, a probable game plan for the next year as well as the next 3, 5, 10, and 20 years.

2. Fully explain, orally and in writing, a proposed investment and wait for you to feel comfortable with it before having you plunk down your money.

3. Welcome questions from you and provide easily understood answers.

Where to find a financial advisor

There are a lot of people out there who want to give you financial advice. How can you determine the qualifications of a good financial advisor? A good place to start is to ask your accountant and attorney. You may want someone who has earned the designation of Certified Financial Planner (CFP),

Chartered Financial Consultant (ChFC) or a CPA/Personal Financial Specialist.

And, remember, an advisor recommends investments geared to meeting *your* objectives—not the other way around.

10.

When to start building your nest egg

We're all on a journey headed for retirement. You can be a tortoise or a hare but you may end up needing to be a cheetah if you don't start saving for retirement now.

It's not really a question of when to start building your nest egg. If you are a baby boomer, you should have *already* started. It's really how much do you need to save each year once you get serious about building your nest egg.

To have a comfortable retirement, you generally need between 60 and 100% of your pre-retirement annual income.

You will not be able to retire just on Social Security benefits. For most people, Social Security will supply about 20 to 40% of pre-retirement income.

If Social Security supplies about 20% of your needed retirement income, where will you get the balance to have 60 to 100% of your pre-retirement annual income? There are four possible sources:

1. Your company's retirement plan (or your own plan if you're self-employed)

2. Your personal savings and investments

3. Working in retirement (this could take the fun out of retiring)

4. Receiving an inheritance (don't count on one since you never know what financial and health problems are

ahead for a person who plans to leave you an inheritance).

Five factors affecting the starting date

The amount of time you have to build your nest egg depends upon five key factors:

1. The earlier you want to retire, the more you need to save now.

   The sooner you retire, the less time you have to accumulate a nest egg. That means you need to save more each year. Also, when you retire earlier, you are giving up a salary and extra years of contributions to retirement plans and dipping into your nest egg sooner.

2. The later you start saving for retirement, the more you need to save each year once you get started. Your savings will have less time to grow through compound interest.

3. The higher the percentage of pre-retirement annual income you want for retirement (e.g, 100% rather than 60%), the more you need to save now.

4. The longer you'll live in retirement, the more you need to save now.

   The size of a nest egg that needs to last until age 95 has to be larger than one to last to age 75.

5. The higher the inflation rate in the future, the more you need to save now.

11.

The benefit of a good foundation

As you'll see in the following example and table, if you already have a retirement plan with one year's salary in it, it will be far easier for you to accumulate your desired nest egg.

Let's look at 10 friends who all want their nest eggs to produce 70% of their pre-retirement annual income. Each of them expects Social Security to supply 20% of their 70% goal, leaving them with the job of funding the 50% difference (70% goal less 20% from Social Security). They each expect to live 30 years in retirement. They're all assuming that the growth on their nest egg savings until they retire will outpace inflation by 6% per year (i.e., if inflation is 3%, then their investments will earn 9%, which is 6% more than the 3% inflation).

The table shown below gives a rough estimate of the percentage of salary each friend needs to save every year if each one has no current savings or has retirement savings equal to one year's salary.

No. of years to retirement	Percentage of salary to save if no savings	Percentage of salary to save with one year's salary in savings
10	60%	47%
15	30%	21%
20	22%	13%
25	15%	8%
30	10%	3%

See how this table applies to these 10 friends—5 of them with no current savings and the other 5 with retirement savings equal to one year's salary.

10 years to save until retirement

Al and Jasmine want to retire in 10 years. Al needs to save 60% of his salary each year for the next 10 years because he has no savings. Jasmine needs to save 47% of her salary each year because she has already saved one year of her salary. Al and Jasmine feel they either need to find a magic genie or inherit from a king to reach their goals.

15 years to save until retirement

Ralph and Alice want to retire in 15 years. Ralph needs to save 30% of his salary each year for the next 15 years because he has no savings. Alice needs to save 21% of her salary each year because she has savings equal to one year of salary. When Alice told Ralph how much more he needed to save than her, he said "to the moon, Alice, to the moon."

20 years to save until retirement

Ben and Jerry want to retire in 20 years. Ben needs to save 22% of his salary each year for the next 20 years because he has no savings. Jerry needs to save 13% of his salary each year because he has savings equal to one year of salary. Ben and Jerry took another look and decided they already have enough to retire now. It's the other Ben and Jerry who have to keep working for 20 years.

25 years to save until retirement

Thelma and Louise want to retire in 25 years. Thelma needs to save 15% of her salary each year for the next 25 years because she has no savings. Louise needs to save 8% of her salary each year because she has savings equal to one year of salary. Thelma and Louise are reconsidering whether they'll live 25 years before retiring, let alone 30 years in retirement.

30 years to save until retirement

Bill and Hillary want to retire in 30 years. Bill needs to save 10% of his salary each year for the next 30 years because he has no savings. Hillary needs to save 3% of her salary each year because she has savings equal to one year of salary. Hillary has mixed feelings that she'll be able to invest her money in a conservative manner and still reach her goal.

Summary

The benefit of having one year's salary in savings or in a retirement plan is tremendous. It can greatly reduce the amount and percentage of salary to save each year during the remaining years until retirement. Again, it's the power of compound interest that makes the difference.

12.

Learning new retirement math: how to calculate the right-size nest egg

Now that you see the wisdom in saving for retirement, you need to learn some new math—"new retirement math," that is.

New retirement math is calculating how much you'll need to accumulate between your company's retirement plan and your personal savings and investments by your retirement date in order to supplement Social Security retirement benefits and live out the rest of your life in comfort and security. If you can't stand looking at any numbers, then at the very least remember this general rule for building the right-size nest egg: you should save *no less* than 10% of your income every year.

How to calculate the right-size nest egg

There are, however, calculations and financial projections you (and your financial advisor) should do to pinpoint the size of your nest egg. You need to know what's behind the numbers.

Every financial projection is a series of assumptions. A small change in an assumption such as the future rate of return (growth) or the inflation rate can have dramatic effects. Whenever you review a financial projection, ask the preparer of the data whether the preparer used "optimistic," "pessimistic" or "realistic" assumptions. Always ask to see separate calculations based on these three types of assumptions.

Translating this to nest egg planning you should see different calculations with a range of different assumptions such as:

1. A long-term annual rate of return of 4%, 6%, 8%, 10%, and 12%
2. An inflation rate of 3%, 4%, 6%, and 8%
3. Retirement income equal to 60%, 80%, and 100% of pre-retirement income
4. Your income staying the same until retirement, going up 2% or 4% per year
5. A retirement age of 62, 65, 67, 70 or 72
6. Life span after retirement of 10, 15, 20, 25, 30, 35, or 40 years
7. No inheritance by retirement age or a possible inheritance based upon your parents' asset situation.

Although there are tables on pages 43 and 44 to show you sample calculations to reach desired nest eggs, it doesn't do you a service to let you think any one table has the right answer for you.

Ideally, you and/or your financial advisor should use a computer program (some are listed in the Appendix) to do different nest egg calculations using various assumptions to pinpoint your needs.

How can you predict the future of the economy?

Even though no one can predict the future, we usually look to the past in trying to decide what inflation, interest rates and rates of return on investments will be like down the road. We get a certain comfort in knowing history, including financial history, which helps us make educated guesses about the future.

The Great Depression started in 1929. If you look at investment returns since 1926, three years before the start of the Depression, there are some interesting results.

During the more than 70 years since 1926, stocks have averaged a compounded annual return of about 10%. During the same period, long-term interest rates and bonds have averaged about half of that.

Within any given year as well as any 10-year period, each of these types of investments has often suffered tremendous losses as well as enjoyed startling gains.

Every financial projection for retirement benefits and education costs in this book (and outside of it) is just an estimate but is based on observations about the past.

Effect of inflation

Let's see how different assumptions about rates of inflation could affect your nest egg.

Inflation has averaged 4% over the last 40 years. Over the last 25 years, it has averaged almost 6%.

After 18 years of 4% per year inflation, a dollar is worth just 50¢. After 36 years of 4% per year inflation, a dollar is worth just 25¢.

After 18 years of 8% per year inflation, a dollar is worth just 25¢. After 36 years of 8% per year inflation, a dollar is worth just 6¢.

If your income and resources do not grow with inflation, your buying power will be diminished to a substantial degree.

The U.S. Treasury has started to issue "real bonds." These bonds guarantee a certain return plus an inflation factor. Talk to your financial advisor as to whether a portion of your investments should be in real bonds.

13.

Eight ways to make sure your retirement investments are right for you

You should not skimp in spending for a crystal ball to predict the future of your investments. If you find it difficult to get an accurate crystal ball then (1) seek qualified professional advice; (2) cross-check the advice you are given with another financial advisor including your accountant; (3) listen to your gut—if you feel uneasy, the advice you are getting may be wrong, or at least, wrong for you; (4) be prepared to meet people who will promise you the moon but take you to the cleaners instead; and (5) educate yourself. The more reading you do, the better equipped you'll be to avoid costly surprises. So, what are you to do?

Here are eight ways to make sure your retirement investments are right for you:

1. First, determine your pre-retirement and retirement goals and objectives (e.g., how important is it for you to own a house right now, before retirement?)

2. Then, prioritize those retirement goals and objectives with your other goals. Since there is never enough money to satisfy all our needs and desires, you need to know what's most important to you, now and in the long run.

3. Think about how much risk you are willing (and need) to take on to meet your retirement goals and objectives.

Take a peek at the worst-case scenario for each alternative. When you review alternative investment choices, pretend you've made the investments before you actually do so. Take a piece of paper and cut it up into smaller pieces, each labelled with the type of investment and dollar amount of each investment. Put the papers under your pillow and see how you sleep the next week. If you're a nervous wreck from make-believe investments, just imagine how the real thing will affect you.

4. Diversify your investments so all of your nest eggs are not in one basket. Usually, it's not a good idea to buy just a few stocks, or invest in just one mutual fund—it's too easy for your entire financial future to go sour this way. Even if you invest in different mutual funds, see if the investing philosophy differs among the funds; otherwise, you might really be putting nearly one identical nest egg on top of another instead of spreading the risk around the hen-house.

5. Consider the income tax impact before making a decision, including the state tax impact (check with your accountant).

6. Don't let your retirement investments get eaten up by inflation, which can gobble up your investment and the growth of your investment.

   Consider buying U.S. government "real bonds." The interest paid on these bonds is tied to the inflation rate so the impact of inflation on your actual interest income is lessened. Talk to your accountant about the income tax impact before buying these bonds.

7. Before you make an investment, get professional advice and understand what the cost will be to get out of the investment if you later conclude it was a mistake.

8. Have an annual financial checkup with a qualified professional to evaluate your goals, your progress, the effect of new laws and new family or financial circumstances.

14.

401(k) plan do's and don'ts

If you have a retirement plan at work, chances are it's a 401(k) plan. A 401(k) plans delays income tax until the retirement funds are withdrawn. This allows your nest egg to grow each year without the tax person taking a bite during the growing years.

Here are seven do's and don'ts on your 401(k) plan:

1. *Don't say no to free money*

Although you, the employee, put in the lion's share of the contributions, usually your employer will match at least some of your contribution (up to certain limits). Make sure you don't pass up this free money from your employer. Once you reach the matching limit of your employer, you might want to consider making a contribution to a Roth IRA (see pages 53-55) with your next available funds to try to qualify for tax-free income. Then, if you still have some money leftover and your 401(k) allows an additional contribution, you could make another contribution to the 401(k) plan.

2. *Your 401(k) is not an ATM window*

Before you borrow from your 401(k) plan, remember that this is a retirement fund. If this isn't enough to convince you to resist temptation, consider that when you pay back your 401(k) loan, you're using after-tax money to do so.

If you leave your job, get tax advice before any retirement plan distribution is made to learn the income tax consequences of the different distribution choices and how loans taken against your retirement benefits should be handled.

Remember, the idea is make your 401(k) a tax-advantaged vehicle, not a tax cow for the government.

3. *Avoid early withdrawals that incur penalties*

If you're not careful, early withdrawals will cause you to owe income tax on the amount withdrawn plus a 10% federal penalty. Ask the plan administrator about rolling over distribution amounts directly to another retirement plan administrator without having the benefits touched by you or taxed to you.

4. *Mix and match your 401(k) investments*

Make sure your retirement plan is not too top-heavy in any one company or industry. Balance risk with growth opportunities and how much time you have until retirement age to recover from any unfortunate investment decisions. The more time you have to recoup, the more risk you can afford to take.

5. *Changing jobs and dealing with your 401(k) can be complicated*

If you had a 401(k) at your old job, you may be able to leave the money there, cash it in, transfer it to a new employer's 401(k) plan or roll it over to an IRA. If you roll it over to an IRA, don't count on being able to put it back into another 401(k) unless you rolled it into a special IRA known as a "conduit IRA." Ask your accountant about the details.

6. See if you can control who inherits the 401(k) if you die before your spouse

Ask your attorney whether you can make sure who inherits your 401(k) (or your spouse's 401(k) if you die before your spouse). Also, discuss whether you want your surviving spouse to be able to change the ultimate beneficiary after your death due to unforeseen circumstances that may occur down the road.

7. 401(k) investments require your attention

At least once a year, look with your accountant or financial advisor at how your 401(k) investments are doing and whether they're meeting your long-term goals. With the federal income tax rules, you generally want (i) high dividend- and interest-paying investments inside your 401(k) and (ii) growth, long-term capital gain type investments outside your 401(k) to minimize the ultimate income tax bite. Your accountant can advise you as to what is best for your particular situation.

15.

The federally insured surprise: retirement assets in banks may not be fully federally insured

You probably know that mutual funds are *not* federally insured. When you invest in a mutual fund, you are depending upon your common sense and governmental regulators to be sure any given fund is kept in line.

However, you may think that *all* retirement funds in banks are *completely* federally insured. Not so. The maximum federal insurance limit on bank deposits for IRAs, Keogh plans, and 401(k) plans is currently $100,000. That's $100,000 total per bank and not $100,000 per type of plan.

Whether you have one or more of these types of plans, you should always confirm the Federal Deposit Insurance Corporation limit for your funds in bank accounts. The solution currently is to keep under the $100,000 FDIC limit in any one institution.

Even if you do not have $100,000 in retirement funds in a bank now, you might in the future. And even if you will never have $100,000 in such plans, you still could be affected if the regulations lower the insured limit in the future. There are also rules on the $100,000 limitation for non-retirement accounts, too. So, at least every year, have your banker confirm the federally insured limits for your retirement plans and other accounts at the bank.

16.

The new IRA game

There have been so many changes to IRAs that you literally need a scorecard to keep track. There's the traditional IRA, the homemaker IRA, the new Roth IRA and the new Education IRA (see pages 105-106). Since the eligibility rules differ with each type of IRA and the rules may change from year from year, always check with your tax advisor as the current requirements and benefits and the state rules, too.

Choose a traditional IRA or a Roth IRA?

The IRA decision process just got a bit more complicated. One important factor to note is that the combined contribution to a traditional IRA and the Roth IRA *together* cannot exceed $2,000 per year per person. You can, however, contribute to the Education IRA (see pages 105-106) on top of these IRAs.

How do you know whether the traditional IRA or the Roth IRA is the right IRA for you? The first step is check the eligibility requirements for each IRA. Then, you need to compare the current and future tax benefits of the "maybe get a deduction now but pay ordinary income tax later traditional IRA" vs. the "don't deduct now, probably get income-tax free money later Roth IRA." Please note that in some cases, the net result to you may be the same with either the traditional IRA or the Roth IRA—your financial advisor and/or CPA has to run the numbers for your situation. And, you may want to use the Vanguard IRA Worksheet on their Internet Web site (http://www.vanguard.com) to help you decide which kind of IRA is best for you.

Traditional IRA

Bottom line: You may be able to deduct contributions now from income but you may pay ordinary income tax (15% to 39.6% on the federal level) on the distributions.

Early distributions will also be subject to a penalty unless they qualify as an exception (always ask your accountant as to the current exceptions since these rules may change over time).

Check with your accountant as to your eligibility to contribute to a traditional IRA.

Roth IRA

Bottom line: You will not be able to deduct the contributions from income but you'll probably pay no income tax on any distributions (including the growth and earnings on your contributions).

Distributions from a Roth IRA will be federal (and maybe state) income tax free if all requirements are met. Early distributions will be subject to a penalty unless they qualify as an exception.

What's better: a traditional IRA or a Roth IRA?

It depends. The potential benefit of the Roth IRA is that all of the distributions may come out federal income tax free (unless Congress changes the rules of the game down the road) and possibly, state income tax free.

The younger you are, the more sense it makes to consider a Roth IRA. A Roth IRA also becomes more attractive the longer you delay taking distributions from it. If your income tax rates in retirement are expected to be higher than your current tax rates, that's another reason to look seriously at the Roth IRA.

Traditional IRAs require distributions to begin at age 70½. Roth IRAs are not subject to this requirement so they can grow income tax-free, possibly for generations.

As with the traditional IRA, eligibility requirements must be met to contribute to the Roth IRA (more people will qualify for the Roth IRA).

At the time this book is being written, you can withdraw your Roth IRA contributions (but not the growth or earnings) at any time without the 10% penalty or income tax being due (withdrawals are considered to come first from your contributions). Always check with your tax advisor before making a contribution or a withdrawal since the rules may change over time.

The Roth IRA rollover

Traditional IRAs may be rolled over into the new Roth IRA if all the requirements are met. The rollover will generate a tax at the time of rollover (which if made in 1998, may be spread out over four years) but then allow the remaining amount and all of the future growth to be paid out federal income tax free (if all the requirements are met). Consult with your accountant to see if this rollover makes sense for your particular situation and to determine where the funds will come from to pay the rollover tax (you probably won't want to dip into the Roth IRA to pay the rollover tax). Also, before withdrawing any funds from a qualified retirement plan as the first step in completing a traditional IRA to Roth IRA transfer, make sure the retirement plan is up-to-date and fully qualified to avoid an income tax surprise.

17.

Eight ways to reduce your income taxes

Since no one likes to pay income tax on top of Social Security tax, it makes sense to take a look at ways to help minimize income taxes.

1. Invest in qualified retirement plans, especially where your employer matches at least part of your contribution

Consider sheltering your income and the return on your investments by investing in qualified retirement plans. Also, if your employer offers matching contributions in a 401(k) plan, this may be your best opportunity for long-term saving.

2. Maximize tax-free income

The higher your income tax bracket, the less you pocket on taxable income such as bank interest and stock dividends. It may pay for you to switch a portion of the investments held in your personal name (i.e., held outside an IRA or other retirement plan) into tax-free income such as municipal bonds from the state in which you reside (especially if your state income tax rate is high). Tax-free means the income is not subject to income tax.

For example, if you're in a 39.6% income tax bracket, a 4.5% *tax-free* investment can net more than a 6.62% *taxable* investment. What this means is that a 6.62% return on an investment taxable at the 39.6% bracket is the same as a 4% return on a tax-free investment. Before you lock into such investments, you should ask your tax advisor about all the tax and financial ramifications of taking such a course of action.

The 1997 tax act created a new type of IRA known as the Roth IRA. Although you do not receive a deduction for putting money into this type of IRA, if all the requirements are met, then all withdrawals (even the growth on your contributions) are free of federal income tax.

3. Avoid having tax-free investments in tax-deferred retirement plans

Generally, tax-free investments (such as *municipal bonds*) earn less than taxable investments. The reason is that you are receiving an additional benefit due to the income being free from income tax (federal, state, or both as the case may be).

Income inside a tax-deferred retirement plan is not subject to income tax while it's in the plan. Income tax is paid when distributions are taken out.

So, all things considered, you do not want to have lower-return tax-free investments inside a tax-deferred retirement plan since your investments will earn less with no compensating tax benefit.

4. Maximize long-term capital gain income

Federal income tax on gain from *ordinary income* can be as high as 39.6%. Compare this to the 8 to 20% maximum federal income tax on most long-term *capital gains*.

An example of ordinary income would be dividends on stocks or interest on savings or bonds. This type of income, under current federal income tax law, can be taxed at up to 39.6%.

An example of long-term capital gain would be the growth in value of a stock held long enough to qualify for this income tax benefit. This growth, under the 1997 tax act, will generally be taxed at an 8% to 20% rate. Since long-term capital gains (e.g., gain on the sale of stocks held for a long enough period) is taxed at a lower federal income tax rate than interest or dividend income, consider investments that produce long-term capital gains. However, first talk to your accountant and/or financial advisor about how the government may tax such gain under the *alternative minimum tax.*

In certain cases, you may get favorable capital gain treatment by *not* rolling company stock from a retirement plan into an IRA. You and your heirs may be income tax and estate tax dollars ahead in the long run by instead putting the stock into your individual name. Although there will be some income tax due right away by doing this, have your accountant run the numbers to see how beneficial this technique might be in your case.

Also, if your employee benefits include income tax-favored options to purchase stock, ask your accountant how the capital gains tax and alternative minimum tax will affect you.

5. Consider a stepped-up basis before you sell assets

A sale of assets while you are alive may cause more or less income tax than a sale after your death. Ask your accountant about the income-tax basis rules when there is a death. Assume you are very ill and are considering selling assets held in your personal name (and outside any IRA or retire-ment plan) to make things simpler for your heirs. There could be a tremendous amount of pent-up capital gain in your assets (e.g., a stock you paid $50,000 for is now worth $200,000). If you sell now, there is income tax to pay on the gain. If, instead, your heirs inherit the assets and they sell the assets, their starting point for federal income tax gain or loss is what the assets were worth on the date of your death

($200,000 in this example). The difference can amount to tens or hundreds of thousands of dollars in unnecessary income tax from a sale during your lifetime. Remember, however, with assets in retirement plans, there is no step-up in basis at death.

6. Consider variable annuities

If you have maxed out your retirement plan opportunities, you should compare *variable annuities* and other tax-free choices with investments that generate long-term capital gains tax (No. 4 above) or no federal income tax (the Roth IRA in No. 2 above).

With your left-over taxable dollars (if there are any), you can invest in annuities in a way that allows growth without income tax until distributions are taken. There is no limit on how much you can invest but you will not receive an income tax deduction for the contributions you make to the annuity. You are using after-tax dollars to fund such an investment. If the investments don't work out, your variable annuity will be reduced accordingly (that's why it's called a variable annuity).

Before you go ahead with such annuities, however, discuss with your tax and financial advisor whether investing in stocks and/or mutual funds outside of a variable annuity would produce a better result. Gains from stocks and/or mutual funds that are invested in your personal name rather than as part of an annuity may qualify for the 8% to 20% long-term federal capital gains tax (if the investments are held long enough) as compared to the potentially higher ordinary income tax rate on annuity payouts. On the other hand, your ordinary income tax bracket may not be as high as it is now when you cash in your annuities. Also, remember that annuities usually have charges ("forfeitures") if you cancel ("surrender") the policy before many years have gone by. See page 63 for a definition and further discussion of annuities.

7. Consider tax credits

Ask your financial advisor how tax credits may reduce your income tax bill.

8. Improve your record keeping

There are two main areas for which you'll want to keep financial records on investments: (1) improvements to your residence that reduce the amount of income tax when you sell your house (see pages 193-194) and (2) stock and mutual fund investments (see pages 195-196).

With stock and mutual fund investments, better records can reduce income tax gain by allowing you to track which portion of your investment can be sold to produce the least amount of gain and which portion has already been taxed (e.g., capital gain distributions that are reinvested).

18.

Saving taxes on distributions from retirement plans

Distributions from retirement plans can be subject to income, death and penalty taxes. There are usually ways to minimize the impact of all of these taxes if steps are taken in advance to plan for them.

Avoiding unnecessary income tax

If you aren't careful, you'll pay an unnecessary 20% income tax on a retirement plan distribution you intended to *roll over* (i.e., put into another qualified retirement plan).

This tax very often comes about if your employer is down-sizing (or now euphemistically known as "right-sizing") and your retirement benefits are transferred out of your former employer's retirement plan. Your employer might ask you a simple question, "Do you want the money sent directly to you?" and innocently enough you respond, "Sure." You can, in fact, avoid this tax by not touching the retirement plan distribution even for an instant.

Instead, have the distribution go directly into an IRA rollover or another *qualified plan* (see if the new employer's plan allows you to do so from day one on the job).

If, instead, your retirement plan benefits are distributed directly to you and, in turn, you immediately put the distribution into an IRA or your new employer's plan, the IRS requires 20% of the distribution to be withheld from you (and paid to the IRS). In addition to this 20% withholding, you will pay income tax on the withheld portion (plus a 10% penalty if you are under age 59½). Always get professional advice before retirement benefits are distributed.

Withdrawals and later returning to the same employer. You may want to leave your retirement account in your former employer's retirement plan. If you leave the company, withdraw your retirement account and later return to work for the same (or related) company, you may not receive credit under the retirement plan for your first work stay. Take a look at the company's Summary Plan Description (see pages 16 and 17) and obtain advice before taking a distribution.

Rules for withdrawal of retirement funds. You may have a choice as to whether your retirement plan benefits are paid out to you in one lump sum or over a period of time (or for the duration of your life or until both you and your spouse pass away). Each type of distribution has income tax consequences. In some cases, you may be able to reduce the income tax due on distributions if you make a special "income tax election" on your income tax return. Ask your accountant about the alternatives available to you.

Beneficiary designations. Talk to your accountant and attorney about how you should complete your beneficiary designation forms to save and/or defer income and death taxes on retirement plan distributions. In some cases, distributions can even be stretched out over time for your children so that they can have a tax-deferred nest-egg growing for decades.

How to take money out early and avoid penalties

Generally, early withdrawals (before age 59½) from retirement plans and IRAs are subject to a penalty. However, ask your accountant about the exceptions.

19.

Living long and in comfort: look to annuities

Besides trying to predict long-term investment returns and inflation rates, baby boomers need to make some educated guesses about their life expectancy and future health condition. How long are you going to live? To age 75? 85? 95? 105?

Have you planned for your money to last as long you do? If not, you should consider investing in an *annuity*.

An annuity is a contract to pay you an amount of money. It's very often a promise by an insurance company to pay you as long as you live.

Even if you have a company retirement plan, IRAs, personal savings and investments and Social Security to count on, you may want to supplement your retirement income with an annuity.

The difference between an annuity and a nest egg

There's a difference between building up a retirement nest egg and having an annuity that will pay as long as you live.

In the past, many company pension plans provided employees with a guaranteed monthly payout that was a percentage of the employee's salary (i.e., it lasted an employee's lifetime and possibly for the lifetime of the spouse of the employee as well). This made it easier for retirees to plan for the future.

During the last decade, employers have tended to drop these pension plans and instead have substituted 401(k) plans. 401(k) plans don't provide a monthly payout related to a percentage of your salary—instead they allow for a tax-deferred buildup of a nest egg and it's anyone's guess as to how long that nest egg will last in retirement.

401(k) plans call for *the employees* to pay all or most of the contributions to the plans. A 401(k) plan has no definite time span as far as payouts—it might last your lifetime or it may run out during your lifetime. You may need to supplement a 401(k) plan with an investment that will be around the rest of your life, such as an annuity.

How should you approach purchasing an annuity? First, see if you have a need for an annuity as part of your retirement planning. If the answer is yes, then you should talk to at least two qualified professionals about annuities. Annuities come in many shapes and sizes. Usually they are sold by insurance companies through agents, stockbrokerage houses or banks. Have the professionals critique each other's proposed annuities (at no cost to you).

Do you need an annuity?

Your need for an annuity at retirement will depend upon the composition of your assets, your personal circumstances, income flow, expenses, life span and future health status, and inflation rates during your lifetime.

At retirement age, perhaps your biggest expense through the years, your mortgage, will be behind you. But will nursing home expenses be the substitute? (See No. 48 and No. 49 on pages 149 through 156 for ways to insure for these expenses.)

Usually, the following expenses go down in retirement: mortgage, personal debts, income and Social Security taxes, life and disability insurance (which are very often discontinued), medical insurance, food, clothing, furniture, and transportation.

Usually, the following expenses go up in retirement: property taxes and rent, house repairs/maintenance, long-term care insurance, and vacation/travel expenses.

Anatomy of an annuity

Annuities, like many investments, can be complex. Since we all can hear sales presentations differently, you should always get a written summary spelling out the critical elements of any proposed annuity before signing on the dotted line.

Since this is an investment that is to last a lifetime, it's very important that the company issuing the annuity (which is a promise to pay you money) be of sound financial strength. There are various rating services (Best, Moody's, Standard & Poors, Weiss Research and Duff & Phelps) that rank insurance companies according to their financial integrity and claims paying record. You should always see these ratings.

There are other factors to consider, too.

How long will the annuity last? Will the annuity pay *(a)* to age 65, *(b)* as long as you live, *(c)* a fixed term (e.g. 10 years), or *(d)* a combination of the above (e.g., for your life but no less than 10 years so that if you die early into the distribution period, your heirs will receive up to 10 years' worth of payments)?

Some annuities allow early withdrawals without any forfeiture if (1) rates of return fall below a certain minimum, (2) you withdraw no more than a certain percentage (e.g., 10%) per calendar year, or (3) you enter a nursing home—please note that the IRS would not be as forgiving and would charge you a penalty for an early withdrawal for any of these reasons (check with your accountant).

financial benefit or detriment of paying off your loan early? Second, what is the psychological benefit you'll receive if your home is debt-free at retirement age or earlier?

Financial considerations

If your house is not worth much more than your loan, it may not be a good idea to pay extra money on the loan.

If you do not pay off your mortgage early, you will probably get an income tax benefit from deducting the mortgage interest on your income tax return. This reduces the real cost of your mortgage payments. Have your accountant explain the income tax rules that may limit, however, the actual benefit of mortgage interest deductions, especially with refinanced loans.

If you do not pay off your loan early, you will have more money to invest. But will you invest that money to receive a greater benefit than paying off your loan early?

If you pay off your loan early, will too much of your net worth be tied up in your house, which is an illiquid asset (i.e., hard to turn into cash immediately)? Also see No. 40 on page 133 and No. 47 on page 146 for additional information.

If you have a 30-year loan, there are three ways to make extra payments to reduce the length (and cost) of your 30-year loan. One way, the hardest way, is to come up with one extra monthly payment each year so that you actually make 13 monthly payments per year instead of 12 payments per year. A second way that may be available through your lender is to let you make payments every two weeks so you still end up making 13 monthly payments but you do it through 26 bi-weekly payments. The third way is just to pay something extra every month (e.g., $100) with your regular mortgage payment, ideally through an automatic withdrawal from your checking account. That reduces your principal balance by that extra amount ($100) per month.

The following four examples show the effect of various payment schedules and assume that there is a $100,000 fixed-rate loan that is taken out (or refinanced) when you are 40 years old.

Example One: 30-year loan at 8% interest with no extra payments

360 payments (30 years times 12 payments per year) of $734 each for a total of **$264,240** ($100,000 principal plus $164,240 interest paid on the loan).

Example Two: 30-year loan at 8% interest with no extra principal payments but with payments made bi-weekly rather than once a month

593 payments (22 5/6 years times 26 payments per year) of $367 each for a total of **$217,844** ($100,000 principal plus $117,844 interest paid on the loan).

Example Three: 30-year loan at 8% interest with extra $100 principal payment each month

240 payments (20 years times 12 payments per year) of $834 each (the extra $100 going to reduce the principal due) for a total of **$200,160** ($100,000 principal and $100,160 interest) paid on the loan.

Example Four: 15-year loan with no extra principal payments at 7½% interest (the interest rate is usually ¼% to ½% lower with a 15-year loan)

180 payments (15 years times 12 payments per year) of $927 each for a total of **$166,860** ($100,000 principal plus $66,860 interest) paid on the loan.

Summary:

Example One: For 30 years at $734 per month with no extra principal payments, you'll pay $264,240 to age 70.

Example Two: For 22 5/6 years at $367 every two weeks, you'll pay $217,844 to age 63 and save almost $50,000 in interest payments as compared to Example One.

Example Three: For 20 years at $834 per month, you'll pay $200,160 to age 60 and save over $60,000 in interest payments as compared to Example One.

Example Four: For 15 years at $927 per month with no extra principal payments, you'll pay $166,860 to age 55 and save over $90,000 in interest payments as compared to Example One.

This summary illustrates how compound interest can work against you (i.e., 30-year loans) just as it can work for you in saving for retirement.

Some loans have penalties if you pay them off early (*prepayment penalties*). Even loans that have prepayment penalties usually allow you to pay off a certain amount each year without being subject to the penalty. Have your attorney check your loan documents on this matter.

Psychological considerations

In balancing the financial pros and cons, remember that a mortgage reduction plan offers the psychological advantage of making your mortgage go away faster and that can be worth a lot.

21.

Houses and the 1997 tax act in a nutshell

The Taxpayer Relief Act of 1997 rewrote the federal tax book on house sales. If your house was sold before 1998, check with your tax advisor as to the rules applicable to you.

Home sales

Married couples can now avoid federal income tax on up to $500,000 of gain on the sale of their primary residence. Single persons can exempt half that amount. In general, there is a two-year ownership period to qualify but there are exceptions for changes in employment, health or certain other unforeseen circumstances that could allow for a partial benefit.

Unlike the old once-in-a-lifetime exclusion, the new federal law can be used repeatedly as long as the two-year and primary residence requirements are met.

Make sure you're aware of the tax laws in your state so you're not accidentally stuck with a big state income tax bill.

You may need to update your will or trust for your beneficiaries to take full advantage of the $250,000 or $500,000 exclusions. Where the first spouse to die leaves his or her portion of the house in certain kinds of trust arrangements under wills and trusts, that portion of the house may not qualify for the special income tax treatment (so part of the proceeds may be subject to income tax on a later sale). Check with your attorney to see if, instead, the house should be allocated 100% outright to the surviving spouse and not to the trust (after balancing estate tax and income tax considerations).

Divorce settlements as to the division of the home may change due to the 1997 tax act.

See pages 193-194 to learn why you will still want to keep track of improvements made to your house even with the more generous income tax exemption.

22.

Big brother taking care of his own: 403(b) and 457 plans

Section 403(b) plans have many similarities to 401(k) plans. Check with your accountant as to the differences. Chances are Section 403(b) plans will become even more attractive over time for income tax and retirement plan purposes.

Section 457 plans offer certain government employees a variation on 401(k) tax-deferred plans. Although the workers provide the funds for these plans, the workers use before-tax earnings as the funding source (and reduce their current year's income tax bill). The money grows tax-deferred just as with a 401(k) plan. Workers can take the savings with them when they leave their job.

Section 457 plans may have some risk in that the plan funds belong to the government entity until they're paid out to the worker. A fiscal crisis could allow the government entity to dip into the Section 457 plan funds. In California, CalPERS, the California Public Employees Retirement System, is a trend-setter in establishing a more secure system to protect workers against any fiscal problem short of a governmental agency going bankrupt. CalPERS has also reduced the fees charged to workers' accounts to make Section 457 plans even more attractive.

If you're a government worker, ask your plan administrator about the safety and costs of participating in a Section 457 plan.

23.

See the USA with an MSA

An MSA is a Medical Savings Account. It's a combination health insurance/retirement plan vehicle.

Tax deductible contributions are put in the MSA. The funds are invested and grow tax-deferred. Money spent for medical bills is free of federal income tax. Any money not spent to pay medical bills can be used at retirement.

MSAs allow individuals who are uninsured, self-employed or who work for small companies (i.e., 50 people or less), to open up an MSA account together with a high deductible health insurance policy. The funds can be withdrawn at or after age 65 for any purpose without a penalty but they will be subject to income tax. Under the 1997 rules, up to $3,375 for a family ($1,462 for an individual) can be accumulated in the tax-deferred account each year. So, an MSA could supplement your IRAs and 401(k) plans and provide additional retirement income.

However, pay attention to the details of the MSA health insurance coverage so that you're not surprised or short-changed due to the lifetime coverage limits, exclusions under the policy, how the deductible and co-payments are applied or the size of the policy premiums. Buyer be aware!

Remember, MSAs are a gamble. If you stay healthy, it can be a good deal. If you have health problems, you may also catch buyer's remorse.

IMPROVING THE
QUALITY OF YOUR LIFE

24.

Adding value to your life

No matter how your financial bank accounts are doing, are you overdrawn or making regular deposits to your life values account?

Why wait until you retire to transform your life and/or work to make it more meaningful or spiritual?

Ask yourself whether you should be working and earning less but spending more time with your children and/or parents?

And, why wait until your life slows down to help society by volunteering? Check out http://www.servenet.org for a list of organizations in your area that are eager for volunteers.

Have you found your passion or purpose in life? Whether you have or not, sit down with pencil and paper and prepare your life values balance sheet of assets, liabilities, talents and desires. Try to give thanks each day for what has gone well and to learn from what hasn't.

Maybe the best will to leave to your children

It's well and good to be fortunate enough to leave a monetary inheritance to your children.

But the greatest gift you can give to your child or children does not have a monetary value—it has an ethical value. When all is said and done, most of us want ourselves and our children to be good people who make the world a better place.

We don't often take the time to put on paper what values we hold as our ideals. Perhaps the best will to leave to your children is an "ethical will."

Ethical wills date back to biblical times. An ethical will does not have a set format. If you want further direction, there are books that provide examples of ethical wills.

An ethical will tells your children the values you hold deepest, the most important lessons you've learned in life, your favorite sayings, special family expressions and the religious or secular writings you hold dearest to your heart. You might tell of mistakes you've made and, sometimes, even ask for forgiveness. This might be the time to finish unfinished business (the lawyer in me does ask that you show your ethical will to your attorney so that this separate document does not contain material that might upset the apple cart of your monetary estate plan).

You can put your ethical will in writing or on a videotape with a camcorder.

Tell your children and grandchildren what you value the most. What a tragedy it would be if you pass on without sharing with them what is most important to you.

25.

Simplifying your life

Simplification will become a major trend as baby boomers age.

With boomers facing a shortage of time and money, one way of improving one's lifestyle will be simplification.

Reducing paperwork and getting financial control

Here are some first steps in the right direction.

1. Consider automatic payouts for mortgage payments and health insurance premiums as well as automatic deductions from your paycheck or checking account for retirement and college savings.

2. Have an automatic deposit of paychecks.

3. Limit and consolidate the number of investments, mutual funds and retirement plans to a manageable number so your assets are diversified, but not too many in number. Too many small investments can lead to chaos and cause you to give up on trying to monitor what's happening where.

Bargain hunting

Are you ready for senior discounts? If you have a psycological barrier to considering yourself a "senior" at age 50 or 55, just change the word "senior" in your mind to "smarter." Here are a couple of places to start:

1. Join AARP (the American Association of Retired Persons, 1/800/424-3410 or http://www.aarp.org) once you reach age 50. You'll qualify for many discount programs.

2. Take advantage of age 50+ discounts at certain banks and savings loans (and save monthly minimum fees that could amount to thousands of dollars over the years).

Selling your house

Many baby boomers will want to sell their homes to fund a good portion of their retirement nest egg or their children's college education fund. Many will be spurred on by receiving tax-free income (federal law allows income tax free gains of up to $500,000 for married couples and $250,000 for single individuals on the sale of a primary residence that meets certain requirements—your state law may allow this, too.)

The RV option

In the 21st Century, there will be a tremendous growth in the number of baby boomer families purchasing recreational vehicles.

Some will buy RVs to reduce housing costs. Others will be buying RVs to have a more flexible lifestyle. Freedom, reminiscent of the 1960s, will be the attraction for these boomers buying RVs.

Finally, some boomers will be looking for less expensive and more flexible vacations. You can set your own itinerary at your own pace with an RV. Restaurants become an option, not a necessity on the road. Stress can be reduced by avoiding airports and motels, too.

RVs offer an opportunity for busy parents to spend more time with their children and in nature.

The key is to learn about RVs before signing on the dotted line. Consider buying a used RV. You'll probably want to rent a few RVs first to see which features and types you prefer. Make sure you've adequate insurance coverage through your car insurance or credit card company before you drive off the lot.

For a free short video on tips for renting or buying RVs, call the GoRVing Coalition at 1/888/GO-RVing (which is 1/888/467-8464).

You can see a directory of RV rental dealers on-line (http://www.rvamerica.com).

The largest RV rental agencies are Cruise America (1/800/327-7799) with 100 locations across the country and El Monte RV (1/800/367-3687), which has locations in California, Washington, New Jersey and Florida. Once you've rented or purchased an RV, you may want to call the Good Sam Club (1/800/234-3450) which offers discounts for stays at RV parks, insurance and other RV needs.

26.

Larger houses and improving the quality of life for the sandwich generation

As the children of baby boomers grow up, many empty-nester boomers will sell their houses and move to smaller homes or to RVs while still others will add on to or buy larger homes.

There are several factors at work here. First, the children of boomers are not moving out of the family house as quickly as boomers did a generation ago. This is due mainly to economic factors such as the cost of living, including high apartment rental rates, and the competition for good paying jobs for high school and college graduates, which is intense.

Also, more boomers are having home offices as their primary or secondary office. In some cases, boomers are moving to larger homes or adding on to existing homes to have a separate home office for each spouse.

More boomers will be having parents live with them and adding rooms or separate "granny houses" which can be attached to or detached from the family house. In some cases, the parents of boomers will make a "gift" to their boomer children by paying for the room or house addition with income-tax free money from the sale of a primary residence.

This can be a win-win situation where personal needs are met and financial realities are shared between the generations.

As the parents of boomers age, it is often critical for boomers to have their parents close at hand to provide them with needed physical assistance. In many cases, demanding jobs make it difficult for boomers to hop on a plane and be gone for days or weeks at a time to help out their parents physically. Having parents and boomers live together may prove to be a better solution.

Home offices will just add to the flexibility and ability to respond quickly to the needs of the parents of boomers. Today, many families are spread across the country, not always by choice. If multi-generational families can live together (I realize not every family can or wants to) and grandchildren can really get to know their grandparents, an invaluable bond and memory inheritance can be transmitted. And that's one gift the government can't tax or take away.

27.

Becoming a stay-at-home parent can pay off big

Most baby boomer families have two parents working outside the home. As a result, both parents are earning coverage under Social Security for retirement benefits. What is often overlooked is that those parents are also earning benefits for themselves and their family if they become disabled or pass away. These benefits can be significant (see page 12 and pages 201 and 202).

Earning Social Security benefits

A stay-at-home parent who works part-time (a home business is permissible, too) can also earn Social Security benefits for himself or herself and the family. The Social Security *disability* or *survivors'* benefits can be critical in helping the family if a tragedy strikes the stay-at-home parent.

To qualify for these benefits, enough *quarters of coverage* need to be earned (there are different eligibility rules for the various types of benefits). A quarter of coverage is earned by having wages or self-employment income at a high enough level for a given year (the dollar amount can change every year). In 1997, for example, earnings (or profits after expenses of your own business) needed to be at least $670 to receive one quarter of coverage (you didn't have to earn $670 in a particular quarter—it's an annual test). So, earnings (or business profits) of $2,680 over the year 1997 would have earned four quarters of coverage.

A stay-at-home parent working part-time might provide an extra safety net of Social Security benefits to pull the family through a tough time.

The homeschooling option

Some boomer stay-at-home parents are part of a growing trend—homeschooling. There are an estimated two million homeschoolers in the U.S. who come from all parts of society and are not just religious fundamentalists.

The ever-increasing presence of home offices provides the flexibility needed to combine parents working and children schooling at home.

Many parents are seriously considering this alternative for educational, spiritual and, in some cases, financial reasons. These are all concerned parents who recognize the importance of the family and the primary responsibility that parents have in transmitting their values directly to their children.

With kids spending six to eight hours a day at private or public school, plus commuting time and extracurricular activities, a parent's role has become secondary in many cases. By contrast, homeschooling offers the opportunity for parents to be a central part of a child's life.

Homeschooling parents, however, don't have to teach everything. Homeschooling children may have tutors and/or still go to school for certain classes and social activities but the home is the primary learning center (homeschoolers Ben Franklin and Abe Lincoln didn't turn out so badly).

Homeschooling at its best provides a quality education with real-life, hands-on experiences on a daily basis and a rich diversity of learning opportunities. Ideally, homeschooling isn't just taking the school model and bringing it home—it's really "lifeschooling," which utilizes every life opportunity as a learning opportunity. Homeschooling can allow parents to develop better relationships with their children.

What is the real benefit of a second income?

For those parents who feel they cannot give up part or all of a second income by homeschooling, they should another look at how little they really have left financially from a second income after federal and state income tax, Social Security and Medicare taxes, work-related expenses including commuting and child care expenses, and, in some cases, private school expenses.

Also, in some cases, the stay-at-home parent will receive the same amount of Social Security *retirement* benefits (by drawing on the other spouse's work record) as he or she would have received by working and paying into Social Security (*disability* and *survivors' benefits* are discussed on page 86).

Boomer parents are reevaluating how much of their energy and lifeforce is used up at work each day rather than having these resources available for their children.

How much extra does a family net if both spouses rather than one spouse earns income? Take a look at this example of a possible scenario.

Assume one spouse earns $60,000 per year as an employee and the second spouse earns $30,000 per year in his or her own business. How much is really left of the second income?

Take a look at the example on the next page and then do your own life values calculations.

The real second income

Net income of second spouse's business after expenses but before taxes	$30,000
Less federal income tax on second income	(8,400)
Less state income tax on second income	(2,550)
Less employer's and employee's Social Security and Medicare tax if you have your own business	(4,590)
Less commuting and non-deductible (e.g., clothing, meals eaten away from home, etc.)	(2,000)
Less child care expenses	(3,500)
The Real Net Income	$ 8,960

And, if there is private school tuition in addition, the net amount left can evaporate completely.

In the future, home schooling may be on track to becoming as popular as home offices are now. If that's the case, baby boomer parents will regale their children with stories of how in the old days, they actually had to walk to school.

28.

A working retirement

Retirement will be redefined by baby boomers. Ever the trendsetters, half of us baby boomers will have to work during retirement to survive financially and it will become "in" to work during retirement.

With retirement lasting until age 85 to 95, most nest eggs won't have the legs to go the distance. That may be a great turn of events.

Why? Many boomers have been and will continue to be so connected with their careers that they'll always identify their self-worth with working. A retirement that does not include an absorbing hobby or satisfying volunteer work or a part-time business or job to fill the void will lead to illness and deterioration.

Too often in my estate planning practice, I've seen men who've gone from a lifetime of work to a continuum of boredom. The result is usually illness and death within a few years. With most women also working outside the home these days too, this prognosis may become all too common for both sexes. The good news is that there is a preventative cure.

Boomers should start thinking now about a hobby, charity or business they'll want to pursue in retirement. Ideally, it should be something they love and, if a business, can profit from, too. The extra dollars will satisfy psychological and financial needs. And, in these days of right-sizing and downsizing, it doesn't hurt to have a side business right now that you can grow into full-time work before retirement if the need arises.

29.

Life insurance that pays while you're alive and ill

If you or a family member is "terminally ill" or "chronically ill" (as defined in the Internal Revenue Code), there may be a way to convert a life insurance policy into cash while the ill person is alive without being subject to federal (and maybe state) income tax. There are certain requirements, of course, and state laws need to reviewed, too. Your state department of insurance can provide useful information to help you make an informed decision.

There are two main types of lifetime payouts. If the insurance company pays you, it's sometimes called a "lifetime benefit," "living benefit" or "accelerated death benefit" (or "ADB"). See if your policy has an ADB rider or can have one added.

The payouts from the insurance company are usually higher than those from third-party companies. If a third-party company pays you, it's called a "viatical settlement."

These payouts can preserve a dignity of life for the terminally ill person by providing needed funds at a critical time.

In some cases, it can even be used for estate planning purposes by providing funds to make death-bed gifts to reduce the size of one's estate for death tax purposes.

However, it is not always beneficial to cash in a life insurance policy while one is alive. Life insurance proceeds paid instead after a death might be free of creditor's claims.

30.

Who do you trust—with your money...and your life?

When you are incapacitated, more than ever you need someone you can trust to handle your money and other assets. If you don't take steps before an incapacity to name your choice or choices, you're taking quite a chance as to who will be in charge of your assets.

Naming someone to handle your money
while you are incapacitated

If you want to name your choices in advance, you can do so in three main documents: a *nomination of conservator*, a *living trust* and a *power of attorney*.

If you become incapacitated, a court may become involved in the management of your assets through a proceeding known generally as a *conservatorship* (sometimes called a *guardianship*). Whether a court-appointed *conservator* (i.e, a person or bank who becomes the manager of your assets) is required depends upon how title (ownership) reads on your assets and whether you have signed a living trust (and transferred the appropriate assets to it) or power of attorney. You'll probably want to sign a document naming a conservator to handle personal, day-to-day living decisions for you if you're incapacitated.

With some documents (a *living trust* or *power of attorney*), court may be avoided. Your agent, under these documents, is put in charge fairly informally and there is no court supervision as to what is done with your money and other assets. These documents may save a considerable amount in attorney's fees and court costs.

The potential disadvantage with these documents is that there is not a court system looking over the shoulder of the person handling your assets. This may not be a problem if you appoint trustworthy people to handle your assets. One way of hedging your bets is to name two people acting together instead of just one person.

As we and our parents age, more thought must be given to how assets will be managed in the event of incapacity.

Depending upon state law and personal preferences, a power of attorney could include powers such as:

1. Create, amend or revoke trusts
2. Place assets in a trust
3. Deal with the Internal Revenue Service
4. Make gifts or be able to take other actions to save death taxes
5. Change beneficiaries on life insurance and retirement plans

Remember, if you sign a power of attorney, you may be signing the equivalent of a blank check with the powers you are giving your agent.

Conflict of interest

Whenever you name someone in a document to act on your behalf, always think about whether that agent would have a conflict of interest and might act for the agent's best interests and not yours. If you name someone to manage and be in charge of spending your assets and that person is also the beneficiary under your will or trust, might the agent hold back on medical or other expenditures on your behalf with the hope of inheriting more and/or sooner? If so, you need to name someone else to act on your behalf.

Who do you trust—with your life?

What can you do to avoid the prolonging of life if you have a terminal illness and the pain and lack of quality outweigh the benefits? What if you are concerned that medical bills in a futile situation will eat up all your assets?

You need to express your desires before you're unable to speak for yourself. The best way is to have a written document that spells out what you want done and what you don't want done in a terminal illness situation.

There are two basic documents for you to explore: (1) a *health power of attorney* and (2) a *living will* (also sometimes called a *directive to physician* or *natural death declaration*).

A health power of attorney appoints an agent to decide big and small health care decisions if you cannot speak for yourself. The biggest decision, of course, is whether to "pull the plug" (i.e., to be taken off life-support machines). A lesser decision might be to choose between two possible operations (when you're unconscious at the time but not in a life-threatening situation). The living will deals just with the big issue, pulling the plug.

You need to have complete trust in the agent you are naming. You should consider whether that person has any financial conflict of interest. For example, will that person inherit from you if the plug is pulled for you? Since the people you select as your agent usually inherit from you too, you should not rule out those persons just because of their status as a beneficiary. However, keep this possible conflict in mind. Also, be sure that the persons you select do not have personal or religious beliefs that will prevent them from carrying out your wishes.

94

31.

Protecting your privacy

There is too much information out there about everyone.
Personal information accumulates and grows. It's like a
bacteria that can't be killed, only controlled.

It's your responsibility to minimize the exposure of your
financial and personal information to keep undesirables from
using your financial resources and/or identity to their
advantage.

Just say no!

Many times it's unnecessary for you to give out your
birthdate, driver's license number, Social Security number,
credit card number or your mother's maiden name. If you
can't see the absolute necessity for providing *any* of the above
pieces of information (try never to give anyone all of the
above except a credit reporting agency such as Trans Union),
then leave that space blank on a form and ask whether it's
absolutely necessary to provide the private information.

For more information on protecting yourself, you may also
want to contact the Privacy Rights Clearinghouse. The
Clearinghouse offers consumers information on how to protect
their personal privacy (http://www.privacyrights.org or
1/619/298-3396, California). You should consider purchasing
The Privacy Rights Handbook (see page 206 for more
information).

Credit reports

There are three large credit reporting agencies listed below. You can get a free report from them if you live in certain states or if you've been denied credit (or under certain other circumstances). If you don't qualify for a free report, ask the agencies about obtaining a joint report at a reduced cost.

If you're about to buy a house, it's wise to check your credit report and correct any errors before applying for a home loan. Also, if your children are going to apply for loans to pay for college based on your credit, you'll want to clear up any errors which might prevent them from qualifying for school loans. Periodically, it's not a bad idea to see what's shown in all three of your credit reports.

The big three credit reporting agencies are:

Equifax
   1/800/685-1111 to request a copy of your credit report
   1/800/556-4711 to have your name removed from mailings

Experian
   1/800/682-7654 to request a copy of your credit report
   1/800/353-0809 to have your name removed from mailings

Trans Union
   1/800/851-2674 to request a copy of your credit report
   1/800/680-7293 to have your name removed from mailings

Keeping an eye on who's keeping an eye on you

You'll want to see who's looking at your credit files and also receive regular updates of your files from the three credit reporting agencies. American Express has started to offer the CreditAware service (1/800/964-3596) to help consumers be sure their credit reports from the three agencies read the same and are accurate.

MAKING THE KIDS AND STEP-KIDS WEALTHY AND WISE

32.

The right and wrong ways to save for your children's college education

With many baby boomers having children later in life and often from more than one marriage, boomers are facing special challenges as they struggle to save for retirement and at the same time save for their children's college education.

Baby boomers, in general, have been a generation of spenders, not savers. And since boomers are expected to live longer than previous generations, their retirement nest egg may need to last 30 to 40 years. Many boomers are discovering the double whammy of trying to save simultaneously for retirement and for their children's college education.

A child born in 1998 will need around $116,000 to cover all the expenses for four years at a public university. This translates to saving $227 per month from the time the child is born. A more realistic goal per child is to try to save up to one-half of the public university cost—$113 per month. The cost for a child attending a private university is double the amount for a public university. The numbers become astronomical for a family with two or three children.

What's a boomer to do? How can limited resources be split between retirement planning and funding a child's college education?

Before investing one penny for a child's college education, the first step is to determine whether investments should be made in the parents' names or the child's. The consequences of this decision on a child qualifying for college financial aid down the line are enormous. This decision not only affects a child's ability to qualify for college education financial aid, it can also have income tax, death tax and other implications.

There are five basic sources for paying for a child's college education: (1) scholarships, (2) the child's earnings while going to school, (3) the child's savings, including any Education IRAs, (4) the parents' savings, and (5) financial aid. In most cases, it will take a combination of two or more of these sources to fund a college education.

The fifth source, financial aid, is very dependent upon the amount of a child's savings and, to a much lesser degree, the parents' savings, assets and income. Prior to opening up savings accounts and purchasing stocks, bonds and life insurance policies to fund a college education, you need to look at the long-term consequences of these actions.

Save in your name?

The key decision is whether you should save college money in your name or your child's. You should make this decision as early as possible since it affects qualifying for college education financial aid and has tax implications, too.

Currently, colleges require students to spend much more of their money (over 33%) as compared to their parents' money (less than 10%) to pay for college education. This makes sense since students should pay to the extent they are capable of doing so. This approach will also make many parents set up a college savings fund in their names rather than their children's.

Another incentive to invest in your name is the income tax benefits with certain U.S. Savings Bonds. If these bonds are purchased in your name, used to pay for your children's college education and your income does not exceed certain limits, you can exclude the bond interest from your income for federal income tax purposes. Since this exclusion phases out as your income gets higher, you need to estimate your future income before deciding upon the actual benefit of this approach. You may want to carefully time when you cash in these bonds to maximize eligibility for aid.

To find out what a U.S. Savings Bond is worth at any given time, http://www.publicdebt.treas.gov/sav/savrepor.htm is the Internet address for the government's Internet Web site. You can also write the Bureau of Public Debt, Savings Bond Operation Office, Parkersburg WV 26106-1328 and request PD-3600 ("Table of Redemption Values").

Blended families

One danger of investing in your name, especially with blended families (i.e., children from a prior marriage on one or both sides), is what can happen to the money if the blended family breaks up and a divorce occurs or if you pass away. Will half or more of the "college education fund" in your name that was intended for the education of your children from a former marriage instead be divided up with your current spouse?

Save in your child's name?

When parents put money or other assets in the names of their minor children to pay for future college expenses, they usually do it under the *Uniform Transfers to Minors Act* ("UTMA") or the *Uniform Gifts to Minors Act* ("UGMA").

In general, with UTMA or UGMA, you can retain control as the manager (called the custodian) until the designated age (age 18 or sometimes age 21) is attained by a child of yours.

If you do not take certain steps when you set up the investments and you pass away before a child reaches the designated age, these assets that were "owned" by your child may be taxed in your estate for death tax purposes. You should consult with your attorney on how to avoid that result.

Another risk of using UTMA or UGMA is that once a child reaches the designated age, the child is entitled to receive all of the assets in the account and use them in any manner. Your children may not want to use the funds to go to or stay in college.

One other ingredient has been added to the mixture by the 1997 tax act. The growth of investments may be taxed at the lowest long-term capital gains rates if the investments have been in the child's name (for enough time and the children are in the lowest income tax bracket) rather than in the parents' names. This gives incentive to put college savings into a child's name at a certain point. However, if you want to keep control of the savings as long as possible to see how your child turns out, you might take an in-between course of action and keep the investments in your name until your child graduates from the Kiddie Tax (i.e., turns age 14)—see pages 103 and 104. Then, you and your spouse could start gifting investments over to an UTMA for your child and have the UTMA later sell the investments at your child's much lower tax bracket (potentially as low as 8% for federal income tax). Check with your accountant now and from time-to-time as to the timing and size limits of such gifts so that income tax, gift tax and death benefits are not wasted.

Using trusts

Instead of putting assets in the name of your children, you might want to put some strings on the assets by creating one or more trusts for your children. A trust could allow you to control the use of the funds.

Talk to your attorney about how such a trust could be written and the tradeoffs of this approach. Keep in mind that it will cost more now in attorney's fees to have trust provisions written as compared to setting up UTMA or UGMA accounts. Also, there will be greater legal and accounting costs through the years after your death in connection with such trusts for your children. Finally, the income tax laws on trusts keep changing and currently much more income tax is due on income that is kept in a trust rather than paid out to a trust beneficiary.

Kiddie Tax

Your family may not save income tax even if you try to shift some investments to your children to have them report the income on their tax return. *Kiddie Tax* says that until a child reaches age 14, a portion of the child's *unearned income* (e.g., interest and dividends as compared to wages from part-time work) may be taxed at the parents' federal income tax rate rather than the child's. This reduces the income tax incentive to shift income to your younger children. However, at the time this book is being written, the first $1,300 (that amount can change over time) of unearned income of a child under age 14 still receives preferential federal income tax treatment. To put some perspective on the numbers, to earn $1,300 in one year with an 8% return, an investment of $16,250 would be required. Since it will take more than $16,250 to have a college fund, you need to consider the income tax implications of any college education fund, especially if any of your children are under the age of 14.

If unearned income exceeds the $1,300 per year amount, then the income tax strategies that make sense for a parent probably will also for a child (i.e., investing in income tax-free municipal bonds; delaying maturity dates of U.S. Series EE Bonds until after age 14 unless a child has already elected to report interest on bonds currently; and investing in stock mutual funds or stocks that pay little in the way of dividends and are held for long-term growth). This last technique, investing in stocks and stock mutual funds, has been very successful over the long haul since returns have averaged 10% per year on stocks. And, with stocks and stock mutual funds, since your child will probably be in a lower income tax bracket than you when the shares are sold, the tax bite at that time probably won't be as severe.

If your children are old enough to work in your family business, encourage them to help you out. Besides hopefully building a mutual appreciation for what each of you can do in the workplace, your children's earnings are not subject to the Kiddie Tax. Your children may even decide to open up IRAs with their earnings and be on the way to saving for their own retirement.

The 1997 tax act and getting professional advice

The 1997 tax act has created a dizzying array of options and possibilities. Some of the new benefits have side effects that may lead to a corresponding reduction of another education aid benefit (leaving you no better off). The complexity in this area will probably cause you to seek professional advice. Try to find a tax advisor who is already knowledgeable about all of the options discussed in this section and is not becoming introduced to these topics and educated at your expense.

Education IRAs

The 1997 tax act created Education IRAs that allow contributions of up to $500 per child per calendar year from a child's birth through his or her 18th birthday. So, that's a maximum of 18 times $500 or $9,000 in contributions (by age 18, there might be over $40,000 in this IRA between contributions and growth). Here you're saving in your child's name.

The contributions are *not* tax deductible but the earnings grow income tax free and the withdrawals are not subject to federal income tax or penalties when used for certain college related purposes. If the money is used for another purpose, it is subject to income tax plus a tax penalty.

Not everyone qualifies to set up these Education IRAs. There are limits on the amount of your income (the limits may change from year to year) and state laws may need to be conformed for this tax benefit, too. If your income is too high to establish an Education IRA, maybe your parents qualify to make the contribution. Grandparents are eligible contributors, too.

There are some restrictions. In the same year, money cannot be put away in both an Education IRA and a prepaid tuition plan for the same child.

Also, financial aid will probably be reduced for those persons with Education IRAs. This may also happen where there are traditional IRAs and/or Roth IRAs—be on the lookout for developments in this area.

And, once your child is in college, the Education IRA cannot have a tax-free withdrawal in the same year you want to benefit from the Hope (tax) Credit described below.

Hope (tax) Credits for education

The 1997 tax act also allows certain taxpayers to take tax credits on their federal income tax return (subject to income limits, too) for certain college expenses. Credits, unlike deductions, can reduce income tax dollar for dollar. Credits are better than deductions. In other words, a $1,500 tax *credit* may reduce your income tax by $1,500. A $1,500 tax *deduction* reduces your income tax by $1,500 times your tax bracket (i.e., if you're in the 28% tax bracket, that's 28% times $1,500 for a $420 income tax reduction).

There are limits on the level of your income for you to qualify for this tax benefit (the limits may change from year to year) and state laws will need to conform to allow for this tax benefit, too. This program gives parents an incentive to delay income, if possible, during the first two years a child is in college. Also, the credit may be reduced by scholarships, grants and other benefits.

The credit can be up to $1,500 per year for the first two years of college (that's a dollar-for-dollar tax credit for the first $1,000 of qualified expenses and then one-half of the next $1,000 of qualified expenses for the first two years of college). Starting with the third year of college, there can be an annual credit of up $1,000 (20% of qualified expenses). After the year 2002, the 20% credit can be $2,000 per year up to a lifetime amount of $10,000 for additional years in college.

Since you can't have the Education IRA and the credit in the same year, you'll need to decide between the two benefits. Check with your accountant as to whether the tax credit or the Education IRA will be more beneficial for you.

Other IRAs as sources

Another provision of the 1997 tax act is that traditional IRAs can be used penalty free (but not income-tax free) for educational expenses of children and grandchildren. Of course, then that money would not be available for retirement purposes and the IRA withdrawals would increase your income for financial aid purposes. From time-to-time, double-check the current rules as to whether these IRAs harm your child's eligibility for college financial aid.

Roth IRAs may be used penalty free for educational expenses and also possibly income-tax free (if all requirements are met). If you have a Roth IRA, ask your tax advisor whether you can avoid income tax and penalties by just withdrawing your Roth IRA contributions, but not the growth.

This area is so technical that you should check with your tax advisor before withdrawing money from any source for educational purposes.

Other possible sources

There are a variety of other sources that may be appropriate for you in accumulating college education dollars.

Tuition prepayment plans. One possibility is to sign up for a tuition prepayment plan that guarantees the payments you make will cover tuition expenses regardless of future increases. What these plans do *not* guarantee is admission for your children to the institution of higher learning or, in most cases, whether the state will guarantee the safety of your money if the tuition plan has financial problems. Since you will be paying a fee through a reduced return to obtain this future cost protection, you need to compare the rate of return on this investment (and the institution's rules on withdrawals if you change your mind or your child does not want to go to college) with other forms of investing. Check with your accountant each year to see if the rules allow you to put away money in both an Education IRA and a tuition prepayment plan in the same year.

Life insurance policies. What about a life insurance policy on you that has a cash value building up inside it as a way to save for college? Since term life policies do not have a cash value build-up, you could consider using a non-term life insurance policy (probably a *variable cash value life insurance policy*) that invests in a mutual fund with growth stocks. Consider the risks, however, because if the investments do not work out, you can lose not only your cash value in the policy *but also* your coverage as well. On the other hand, if the investments do work out, you can reduce the size of your premium payments. The value inside such a policy would increase free of any income taxes. At college entrance time you could tap that cash value.

Instead of cashing in the policy to pay for college expenses, you could withdraw the cash value in a non-taxable policy loan to pay for college expenses. If you should die before your children were ready for college, the amount available would be even larger due to the life insurance component of the policy. And, yes, these death benefits could pass income-tax free to your children.

Usually it makes sense to use life insurance only if you need the insurance anyway and there are ten or more years until your children are applying for college since the surrender charges and fees may be too high compared with the return.

Alternative service and other schools

Consider utilizing community/junior colleges and vocational schools as alternative or complementary education sources.

Don't overlook the educational benefits offered in return for service given to our country including military service, AmeriCorps and other national programs.

Student loans. Another source is student loans where some interest may be tax-deductible. Find out how much of the interest can be tax-deductible and for what period of time. These student loans are probably a better source than totally non-deductible credit card loans.

Finding financial aid

Call 1/800/433-3243 for the U.S. Department of Education's guide *Funding Your Education.*

For a wealth of information, take a look at the Web site of the National Association of Student Financial Aid Administrators (http://www.finaid.org).

Home equity loans. As last resorts to be avoided if possible, you might tap into the equity in your home or a retirement plan to raise necessary funds. Ask your accountant about the limits on deducting interest on home equity loans and the possible income tax consequences of early withdrawals from a retirement plan.

Steps to consider while a child is in high school

Usually two or three years in advance of college entrance time, you'll look into changing the form of any higher-risk tuition investment (e.g., certain stocks and mutual funds) into a safer one producing a fixed rate of return (e.g., certificates of deposit).

One way to plan for the conversion of funds automatically is to purchase *zero-coupon municipal bonds.* With these bonds, you pay a discounted price now (e.g., $600) and when the bond matures, you receive the full price ($1,000). Your purchase of zero-coupon bonds can be staggered to mature one-fourth each year for four years. Of course, these days students are not usually graduating in just four years. You might want to build in a fifth year plan, too.

Another approach is to encourage your children to take advanced placement classes and tests to obtain college credit while in high school. This is one way to shorten the college tuition duration. Maybe you could offer your children a financial bonus if they get college credits in high school (e.g., give your children one-half of the savings for the earned units).

As tuition time rolls around, grandparents may want to help out. Although there is a federal gift tax exclusion for gifts of up to $10,000 per recipient per calendar year (the $10,000 will be adjusted for inflation), there are two ways to increase that amount. A grandparent can take care of a grandchild's unreimbursable, qualified medical expenses by making a payment directly to the health care provider (medical insurance comes under this, too) and a grandparent can handle a grandchild's educational expenses making a payment directly to the educational institution. And, a Roth IRA may qualify to be used income-tax free to pay tuition of a grandchild. All in all, grandparents may want to reduce potential death taxes by paying their grandchild's tuition by some of these gift approaches.

If all else fails

All of the these tax benefits for education costs have different eligibility requirements tied to the level of your income. If you still fall short of funds even after utilizing all available benefits and programs, remember that you may be able to negotiate with colleges in paying tuition costs.

33.

Calculating a college-size nest egg

The nest egg for a private university will probably need to be twice as large as one for a public university.

For a student entering college in 1998, the four-year total cost (tuition, books, room and board and other expenses) is around $48,000 for a public university and around $96,000 for a private university. As each year goes by, inflation will probably increase these costs at a 5% per year rate. That means an eight-year old will face public university costs of nearly $80,000 and private university costs close to $160,000.

These staggering costs point up the need to start saving now, even if it means using a piggy bank. The good news is that you can cut in half the amount you need to save if your children go to a public university.

Should you plan to save all of the costs?

It may be unrealistic for you to assume you can save 100% of these probable college costs. Whatever you can save will be a big help. If you can manage to save one-half or two-thirds of the needed amount, you will have achieved a great deal. Any savings you already have in place for college costs will also reduce the monthly amount needed to accumulate the desired college nest egg. Your children may be able to pay for the difference through loans, scholarships or other financial aid, including work-study programs.

The effect of inflation on college costs

The table below assumes your child enters college at age 18 and shows how 5% per year inflation will drive up private and public college education costs.

Your child's year of birth	Total 4-year cost at private university	Total 4-year cost at public university
1980	$ 96,428	$48,214
1981	101,249	50,625
1982	106,312	53,156
1983	111,627	55,814
1984	117,209	58,604
1985	123,069	61,535
1986	129,223	64,611
1987	135,684	67,842
1988	142,468	71,234
1989	149,591	74,796
1990	157,072	78,536
1991	164,925	82,463
1992	173,171	86,586
1993	181,830	90,915
1994	190,922	95,461
1995	200,468	100,233
1996	210,489	105,245
1997	221,014	110,507
1998	232,064	116,032
1999	243,668	121,834
2000	255,851	127,925
2001	268,644	134,322
2002	282,076	141,038
2003	296,180	148,090

The next table shows how much you will need to save each month to reach your goal.

Your child's year of birth	Monthly savings for 50% of public university cost	Monthly savings for 50% of private university cost or 100% of public university cost
1981	$1,909	$3,818
1982	962	1,924
1983	646	1,293
1984	488	977
1985	393	786
1986	330	659
1987	284	568
1988	250	500
1989	223	446
1990	202	403
1991	184	368
1992	169	338
1993	156	313
1994	145	291
1995	136	272
1996	128	255
1997	120	240
1998	113	227
1999	119	238
2000	125	250
2001	131	263
2002	138	276
2003	145	290

The first monthly savings column shows the amount of monthly savings you'd need to reach 50% of the expected public university cost. The second monthly savings column shows both the amount of monthly savings for 50% of the private university cost or 100% of the public university cost—they are the same amount since it costs about twice as much for a private university.

The last table was based on starting to save for college costs from scratch on January 1, 1999, earning 8% per year (before taxes) on the investments and reinvesting all the earnings. However, if your child is born in 2000 or later, then the table assumes you started to save on January 1 of the year in which your child was born.

The earlier you start, the smaller your monthly nut

The last table shows is the benefit of starting to save early. If your goal is to save 50% of the cost of a four-year education in a public university for a child born in 1999, you can achieve that goal under the stated assumptions by saving $119 per month when the child is born. If you delay saving for that same child until the child is three years away from entering college, to reach the 50% public education cost goal you'd need to save around $1,500 *per month* (that calculation is not in the table).

To meet your savings goal, you should try to set up an arrangement whereby funds are withdrawn automatically from your checking account and put into your college fund investments. Each year, you should review with your financial advisor both the rate of return on your investments and the college cost inflation rate to see that you are staying on schedule in your savings program.

34.

Keeping Uncle Sam out of your estate

You can take steps to reduce or eliminate federal death tax and have more on hand for your children. Death tax starts at 37% and goes up from there.

On what size estate is federal death tax due?

For most people, the magic number will be at least $625,000 as to whether there will be any federal death tax. For estates below that size, no federal death tax should be due for deaths occurring in 1998. The 1997 tax act is gradually increasing the $625,000 exempt amount each year to get up to $1,000,000 for deaths in the year 2006 or later.

You should pay attention as to how that $625,000 or $1,000,000 amount is determined. First, add up *all* your assets such as real estate, cash, stocks, bonds, business interests, cars, and personal items. Then, add up your IRAs, retirement plans, and certain life insurance policies (the ones controlled by you) and all of your other assets. Next, subtract your debts and liabilities (such as mortgages, car loans, and personal loans). If the remainder is below the exempt amount, then, in general, there won't be any federal death tax.

Depending upon how a husband and wife set up their wills, trusts and ownership of assets, they could each potentially have a $625,000 exemption in 1998 (and up to $1,000,000 in the year 2006) or a total $1,250,000 million exemption in 1998 (and up to $2,000,000 in the year 2006) for the family.

Let's look at how this could work for a couple worth $625,000 each for a total of $1,250,000 together. This number is not far-fetched for many couples when you realize that life insurance (unless special steps are taken in advance—see below) and retirement plan benefits are part of the equation.

$245,000 in unnecessary death tax

If one spouse worth $625,000 leaves all of his or her assets outright to the surviving spouse (worth $625,000, too), then the survivor will be worth $1,250,000 at the time of his or her death. If the surviving spouse can only shield $625,000 from death tax (upon dying in 1998), then the remaining $625,000 will be taxed. The federal death tax in this scenario would be $245,000. There is a way to keep that $245,000 within the family instead of making this donation to the IRS.

Death tax savings trust

This $245,000 federal death tax could go down to zero on the $1,250,000 in assets if the first spouse to die had set up a will or trust with a *death tax saving trust* (sometimes called a *B trust, credit shelter trust* or *exemption trust*). The reason is that assets of the first to die in a properly drafted death tax saving trust will not be counted as being owned by the surviving spouse. The assets of the first to die would be shielded from death tax by the $625,000 exemption permitted for the first to die (this exemption goes up each year from $625,000 in 1998 to $1,000,000 in the year 2006).

With a death tax saving trust in a will or trust, the surviving spouse could be the beneficiary of the trust and, in some cases, be the trustee (manager) of the trust as well. Your attorney can explain how this type of trust works.

Ask your attorney if there will be state inheritance tax and/or federal and state income tax even if there is no federal death tax.

Ways to increase the federal death tax exemption

If you pass away leaving a surviving spouse and an estate larger than the federal death tax exempt amount ($625,000 in 1998 and gradually increasing over time up to $1,000,000 for deaths in the year 2006 or later), there are ways to leave the excess above the exempt amount ($625,000 in 1998) to your spouse with no federal death tax due at your death. If your will or trust qualifies for the federal *marital deduction*, there may be no federal death tax due at the time the first spouse dies.

Keep in mind that if the assets you are leaving to your spouse qualify for this marital deduction, there may only be a delay, or deferral, of death tax until your spouse dies. The assets that qualify for the marital deduction (or what's left of them at the survivor's death) are then counted in the survivor's taxable estate. This will increase the size of the survivor's estate. For details on the marital deduction, contact your estate planning attorney.

Another way to exempt more than the federal death tax exemption is by making gifts during your lifetime. Only certain kinds of gifts, however, qualify to stretch the exempt amount. So, review any proposed gift with your attorney before making the gift to determine whether it eats into your federal death tax exemption instead of stretching it.

In general, you can make lifetime gifts of up to $10,000 per calendar year per recipient that do not use up any part of your federal death tax exemption. Husbands and wives can usually double these $10,000 amounts if certain technical requirements are met. The $10,000 amounts will be adjusted for inflation after 1998. You can also stretch the $10,000 amount by paying tuition and/or medical expenses directly to providers on behalf of the persons you want to benefit.

It's important to understand the consequences of lifetime gifts before the gifts are made. Some gifts may increase the overall tax to your family. With advance planning, you can sometimes restructure a gift so that it produces a tax benefit you would otherwise have lost. Since states have their own rules on these matters, you cannot ignore state law consequences. Besides lifetime gifts, another way is to shift an "opportunity" (e.g., an investment) to your children well in advance of your death where there is a good likelihood that the opportunity will grow in value.

Also, certain family partnership arrangements and/or lifetime transfers of interests in family businesses or property, including the use of trusts, can reduce the tax bite.

You should review this area very carefully with your estate planning attorney since there are special rules for family transactions.

Finally, consider taking steps regarding life insurance to alter the common result of life insurance being subject to death tax. There are special ways to own life insurance so you can pass on large amounts of life insurance to your children without any death tax due on the proceeds (See No. 58 on page 180). Consult with your attorney on the ways to achieve this result.

TYING OR RETYING
THE KNOT

35.

What you must know before you marry or remarry

Whether you are planning to marry for the first time or get remarried, you need to do some advance planning to avoid some surprises down the road.

You'll want to consider how title (ownership) is taken on assets each of you owns now and may own in the future, such as bank accounts and a house, so that the intended beneficiaries inherit upon a death.

For example, if you own assets with your spouse as joint tenants, your children from a former marriage may get nothing upon your death even if your will leaves everything to them. Why? Because, in general, certain ways of holding title (ownership) such as joint tenancy *override* a will or trust.

How you take title may also impact how assets will be divided in case this marriage (or remarriage) doesn't work out.

Title to assets can also affect income taxes for the surviving spouse and death taxes for the family.

You should sign a new will and/or trust after getting married. If you don't do so, the law will probably assume that you wanted to carve out a sizeable share or all of your estate for your spouse but just never got around to doing so.

You need to think through the provisions of a new will or trust. You might say, "I want to leave everything to my kids from my former marriage." What if your spouse sold his or her residence to move into your house? You may want to provide for your surviving spouse. Would you want your spouse to have to move out right after your death or would you instead allow your spouse some time to live there and plan the next move? Would your spouse be paying rent or taking care of expenses on the residence during that time period? What about the furnishings in the residence? If they had belonged to you, would you want your spouse left without a stick of furniture? Take a look at No. 39 on pages 128 and 129 for additional suggestions in providing for a surviving spouse and protecting your children from a former marriage.

If you have young children, you'll need to think about who should be named as the guardian to raise them.

Coordinate your will and/or trust with the beneficiary designations on your IRAs, retirement plans and life insurance to take advantage of all available income tax and death tax benefits. You should update your will and trust for tax changes, too, such as the 1997 tax act. And, if you or your spouse are not U.S. citizens, make sure your estate plan has all needed special provisions to prevent death tax surprises.

See No. 37 on page 126 to see how your marriage could affect college financial aid.

All of these issues and others such as retirement plan and IRA payouts need to be coordinated in a master plan worked out with your attorney so that no element is working at cross purposes with the rest of the plan. You should review with your attorney, before the marriage, your potential liability for debts of your spouse, including tax obligations.

Before you go to the altar, go to your attorney to discuss the reasons for considering a marital agreement.

Finally, take a look at No. 50 on pages 159 and 160, which discusses considerations for your parents' remarrying because these issues may apply to you, too.

36.

Will Uncle Sam tear up part of your marital agreement?

Assume many years ago you signed a beneficiary designation naming your two grown children from a prior marriage as the beneficiaries on your long-standing retirement plan. Let's say you remarry, and a marital agreement is signed saying what's yours is yours and what's mine is mine, including retirement plan assets. After the remarriage, you sign a new will leaving everything to your children. If this new marriage lasts two years and then you pass away, who will get the retirement assets?

It may be that your surviving spouse will receive all of the benefits through an annuity that lasts for the spouse's lifetime. Why? Depending upon the type of retirement plan, federal law may say that your spouse must be the sole beneficiary because your spouse never signed a necessary *waiver* form after the marriage concerning retirement plan benefits.

This can distort your intended result, especially if the retirement plan is a major asset in the estate. Talk to your attorney about the steps you can take to avoid this confusion.

37.

Filling out college aid applications before and after the wedding

Becoming a step-parent can have quite an impact on a child's or step-child's chance of qualifying for college aid programs.

If you're a single parent, you are not reporting the income and assets of anyone except yourself.

Once you get married (or remarried), you are then part of a team and the financial situation of the entire team needs to be considered.

Federal aid programs consider the income of the custodial parents. If you are not yet married, then your children are not reporting the income of your spouse-to-be. When you and your spouse say "I do," each of you may be saying "I'll pay" for the college education of your step-children when they have a second custodial parent.

That means the financial picture of both parents enters into the equation to determine *eligibility* for college aid, even if you've signed a pre-marital agreement saying each of you will pay for your own children's education. Ask your attorney whether your state law requires a different arrangement.

38.

For better or for worse—what can that *really* mean?

Before you tie the knot, check to see whether Social Security benefits will be affected by your marriage. For example, a divorced person claiming benefits on an ex-spouse's working record could lose those benefits by remarrying.

Before you *un*tie the knot and get a divorce, ask whether you'll qualify for Social Security benefits under your soon-to-be ex-spouse's working record by staying in the marriage for a bit longer.

You also should get advice on your potential liability as a spouse and on ways to protect your assets.

You need to know the implications of putting your new spouse on title to the residence you brought into the marriage. Will the house be sold if your spouse's business venture goes belly up? Will the house be sold due to a debt incurred before the marriage that was never paid off? How will the house be divided if the marriage breaks up?

Finally, will the government force you to use your assets to pay for your spouse's nursing home costs and medical bills even if you've signed a marital agreement saying you'll each pay your own way?

Buy some time for a consultation with an attorney so you can ease your concerns and enjoy your marriage.

39.

Protecting the inheritance for your kids

If you are in your first marriage or a remarriage, there is a way you can benefit your spouse under your will or trust but also make sure your children are the beneficiaries of what's left over after your spouse passes away.

This technique is called a *QTIP* (*qualified terminable interest property*) trust. This type of trust gives you some control over assets left to benefit your spouse. It allows your spouse to benefit from your assets but at the same time gives you the final say as to the ultimate beneficiaries once your surviving spouse passes away (even if your spouse remarries).

The best planning in a will or trust will all go out the window unless you hold title (ownership) to your assets in a way that complements your intended plan. Otherwise, assets may pass outside the will or trust to unintended beneficiaries.

You'll also need to review with your attorney how beneficiary designations on life insurance, IRA, 401(k), and other retirement plans should read after a marriage. You may need to have your spouse sign a special waiver so certain retirement benefits go to someone other than your spouse (e.g., your children from a prior marriage).

If you are remarrying and you and/or your future spouse have children from a former marriage, talk to your attorney about how your will or trust may benefit or exclude step-children. If you don't deal with this issue, it may be that upon your death your state law will give step-children and your children equal shares of your estate. This is fine if it's what you want to happen. But do your family a favor and don't have everyone guessing and paying attorney's fees to sort things out after your death.

Some wills and trusts tie the size of the children's inheritance from a first marriage to the amount of the federal estate tax exemption ($600,000 in 1997). The exemption increased in 1998 (to $625,000) and it will increase each year until the year 2006 (when it will be $1,000,000). If your pre-1997 tax act will or trust says give the maximum exempt amount to the children, would your children receive $600,000, $1,000,000 or something in-between? Have your estate plan reviewed to avoid confusion.

Finally, be sure that your will and/or trust says who will pay death taxes. Otherwise, it could be that your spouse or a child receives an asset outside the will or trust but only the beneficiaries under the will or trust pay the death taxes on that asset. This could result in a total depletion of assets passing under the will or trust.

Instead, it may be preferable that each beneficiary, whether inheriting under your will or trust or receiving an asset through a beneficiary designation, pay his or her fair share of death tax according to how much was received.

MORE WAYS
TO PROTECT
THE NEST EGG

40.

Refinancing for the better

The biggest expense for most baby boomers is their home mortgage. One great way to cut down costs and provide extra funds for retirement and education planning may be to refinance the home mortgage when rates are advantageous. Keep in mind, though, that if you take out a 30-year loan at age 50 and you do not pay additional principal over the years to reduce the lifespan of the loan (see No. 20 on page 69), you could be making large mortgage payments until you're 80-years old.

Also, be aware that if you refinance, there may be a prepayment penalty (see page 72) and not all of the interest may be deductible (check with your accountant). Also see No. 47 on page 146.

There is also one hidden aspect of refinancing that may affect your nest egg in an unexpected way.

When you buy a house and take out a loan as part of the purchase, some states give you special protection in that you may have no personal liability if you do not complete the payments on the mortgage. The lender in those cases may only go against the house and not your other assets to collect on the house loan.

When you refinance, you are probably giving up that protection because the refinanced loan was not taken out at the time of purchase. There may be circumstances where this personal liability potential could affect your decision to refinance. You should obtain appropriate assistance on this matter.

41.

Protecting retirement plan assets

There are four main ways you can protect retirement plan assets. Three of the techniques protect you and one protects your heirs.

First, be diligent concerning the investment of retirement plan assets. More and more you'll see fraudulent, pie-in-the-sky schemes to lure retirement investors.

Second, become aware of the tax rules on different types of distributions and how beneficiary designations can affect the deferral of income tax. Also, by retirement age, you should become aware of how distributions could increase the income tax on your Social Security benefits.

Third, if you own a business, be aware that different types of retirement plans offer different degrees of protection in case you ever need to file bankruptcy. With some types of plans, you may be able to keep the retirement plan assets from going to creditors as part of a bankruptcy. With other types of plans, the retirement plan assets could be totally lost. You should talk to your attorney about the possibilities for your situation.

Fourth, ask your attorney how to complete beneficiary designations to prevent retirement plan assets from going through probate unnecessarily if you die. Probate would result in higher attorney's fees and assets possibly going to creditors instead of your family (see No. 44 on page 137).

42.

Life insurance do's and don'ts

Although state laws generally protect life insurance proceeds from creditors, there is one way that the proceeds can get thrown in the pot and be subject to the claims of creditors: if one's estate is named as the beneficiary on a life insurance policy, then the proceeds may not only have to go through probate unnecessarily but they also can be claimed by creditors, justly or unjustly.

Life insurance money may also end up in your probate estate if all of the beneficiaries you name on the designation form fail to survive you. If you named your parents as the primary and backup beneficiaries on a policy and they both pass away before you, the life insurance proceeds would probably end up in your probate estate. Instead, if you had updated your beneficiary designations, the proceeds could have been paid quickly and correctly to the beneficiaries you had in mind without having to go through probate. (See No. 44 on page 137 for a further discussion of probate).

So, talk to your attorney about how to fill out your beneficiary designations forms. The forms may look insignificant but the choice of a few words can affect generations.

Also, don't assume that life insurance will escape death tax. You need to take special steps as described in No. 58 on page 180.

43.

How to plan for rainy days: umbrella insurance

This is not a society where people are shy about suing.

The usual amount of car insurance doesn't protect you against the major losses that can easily occur.

One relatively inexpensive solution is to have *umbrella insurance* on top of your regular car and home liability insurance. This kind of insurance starts paying when your other insurance coverage is exhausted. You may be able to get up to $1 million, $2 million or more of coverage for far less than you think.

Ask your liability insurance agent about umbrella insurance. That way you may not get soaked when a bit of rain pours into your life.

Is there a gap in your homeowner's, renter's and car insurance?

Your homeowner's or renter's insurance policy may not cover household help, including nannies, nurses and persons working at or on your house. You may not have coverage for an accident caused by a non-family member or other person driving your car. Ask your insurance agent about any potential gaps in coverage.

44.

Avoiding probate with a living trust

Usually when you pass away your estate will go through *probate*. Probate is the legal procedure set up by your state to see that taxes, debts, and expenses are paid and your remaining assets are distributed to the correct beneficiaries or heirs. This procedure is supervised by a court sometimes referred to as the "probate court." Most people associate probate with high attorney and executor fees, delays, and hassles.

One way to avoid probate is to set up and transfer the appropriate assets to a *living trust*. A living trust is a legal document spelling out the management and distribution of your assets while you are alive *and* after you die. The main difference between a will and a living trust is that upon a death a living trust may avoid the probate court altogether.

In general, setting up a living trust provides no protection against creditors. Since you can revoke the trust and maintain total control over your assets, you are still considered the owner of the assets while you are alive. At your death, the assets in the trust are usually subject to claims by your creditors.

One way that may provide additional protection against creditors is holding title in *joint tenancy*. State law will determine if that's the case. Ask your attorney about the tax and non-tax ramifications on holding title in joint tenancy (see also No. 52 pages 162 to 164).

Another way to possibly obtain protection against creditors is to establish an irrevocable (unchangeable) trust. Ask your attorney about the pros and cons of establishing a trust in another state such as Alaska.

Finally, ask about how the relationship between a living trust and eligibility for government aid on nursing home care expenses.

MOVING TO
GREENER PASTURES

45.

Finding the right place for your parents to retire

As a baby boomer, there's a good chance you'll need to help take care of your parents.

Physical proximity to your parents can be of great comfort to them and to you. It can also help you avoid disruptions at work, which is important in these days of job insecurity.

When our parents need us, there's usually a crisis that may linger on for years. With blended families, we may be stretched out literally and figuratively as parents, step-parents, siblings, and step-siblings relocate across the country.

By the year 2004, baby boomers will range in age from 40 to 58. Our parents will be in their 60s, 70s, 80s or 90s, and many of them will need personal care and help from their baby boomer children. Where your parents, step-parents, and other close relatives will be living in relation to you will be important.

There are financial implications relating to where one lives. For example, different states have different rules for determining eligibility for governmental assistance in paying for nursing home costs. Don't assume that because you have become educated about the rules in one state (and that your parents would qualify in that state) that your parents will qualify if they move to another state. This is an important item to be checked out with an attorney before any final decisions are made by your parents.

Qualifying for eligibility can be tricky in two circumstances. First, if your parents live in one state part of the year and in another state the rest of the year, both states could say that your parents need to apply for assistance in the *other* state.

Second, a problem could occur if your parents first move from their home state to another state for retirement, then later return to the original home state and an illness occurs. The home state may try to claim that the true permanent residence is not there, but is instead in the retirement state.

These possibilities point up the good sense of obtaining legal advice on how to sever ties with a state (e.g., voting in the new state, getting a driver's license in the new state, signing a will or trust in the new state, signing a declaration of domicile, etc.) and whether it is advisable to do so.

The ability to pay long-term nursing home costs can thus be affected by where your parents live. For more information, refer to No. 48 and No. 49 on pages 149 to 156.

Your parents will also face the issues described in No. 46 on pages 143 through 145.

46.

Six questions you need to ask before moving to a new state or staying right where you are

Most of us assume we can live anywhere in the United States and the laws and rules will be pretty much the same. As discussed in No. 45 on page 141, the implementation of the rules on governmental assistance for nursing home costs differs from state to state.

There are six questions you need to ask before making a move. Your parents need to get the answers to these questions, too, before they start packing their bags.

1. Will my marital agreement be enforceable in the new state?

A marital agreement valid in one state may not be enforceable if you move to another state. Also, the rules for the necessary elements in the agreement may be different, depending upon whether the agreement was signed before or after the marriage. You might need to sign another agreement in the new state if your spouse is agreeable.

Some states use a community property concept of ownership while most use a separate property approach. Find out whether you'll be affected by a move to a new state.

2. *Will my will or trust work the same in the new state?*

The laws for wills, trusts and inheritance are not identical in every state. Everyone who moves to a new state should have his or her will or trust reviewed by an attorney in the new state to be sure no surprises arise down the line. For example, in these days of blended families, it's important to ask an attorney in the new state what the rights, if any, would be for step-children if you did not revise your will or trust.

3. *Are the income tax laws different in the new state and will I still be subject to income tax in the old state after I move?*

There are different state income tax laws across the country. As you look for a place to retire or decide to buy a house now for the retirement years, you might seek out a state without an income tax. If you earn a pension in a state with an income tax and then move to a state with no income tax, ask your accountant whether income tax authorities of the first state can follow the pension income to the new state to tax it. Congress has passed limitations on the old states taxing pensions in most cases.

4. *Are the property tax laws different in the new state?*

Property tax laws differ across the country. Some states give special property tax breaks to senior citizens. Others allow children to receive special tax benefits if they inherit or receive real estate as a gift.

One state, for example, might allow property taxes to avoid an increase after your death only to the extent your children, and not your grandchildren, inherit real estate from you. With this in mind, you might change your will or trust to allocate your house only to your children and have other assets go to your grandchildren to take advantage of this property tax benefit.

5. Are the inheritance tax laws the same in both states?

Talk to your legal and financial advisor about whether the inheritance tax laws are more favorable in one state as compared to another and whether you should take certain steps (e.g., voting in the new state, getting a driver's license in the new state, signing a will or trust in the new state, etc.) to establish a *domicile* (i.e., permanent residence) to determine where you should be taxed. Also, find out if you can avoid having a probate upon your death in any state, let alone in more than one state.

If you split your time between two or more states, both states may try to take a tax bite out of your estate at your death. Or, one state may have no inheritance tax and the other state may have a steep tax and you can guess which one would like to go after a piece of your estate.

6. Are the health insurance laws the same in new state?

Some states offer more liberal or more restrictive health insurance coverage. Check it out before a move is made.

47.

Paying all cash for your home for retirement may not be wise

When you start thinking of buying your dream home to live out the retirement years, you might want to avoid making an all-cash purchase (even if this luxury is possible).

First, you'll be tying up a large portion of your assets in an illiquid (hard-to-sell) asset by paying all cash.

Second, if you borrow against the property in the future after the purchase is completed, there may be personal liability on the loan you could have avoided by taking out the loan at the time of purchase (see No. 40 on page 133).

Finally, you may not be able to deduct all the interest on a loan taken out after the purchase of a property. Ask your accountant about limitations on deducting interest.

NURSING HOME
NEWS

48.

What your parents should be doing now to avoid going broke paying future nursing home costs

Planning your retirement should include considering the future needs of your parents, which could affect you emotionally as well as financially. One of their greatest needs may be paying for nursing home costs. Probably about half of the parents of baby boomers will need nursing home care.

Nursing home costs can range from $1,500 to $8,000 per month. The costs may be doubled if both parents require this care.

How do the elderly pay for nursing costs now? Some pay their own way and others qualify for governmental assistance through Medicare or Medicaid. Medicare pays for a very small portion of the country's long-term nursing home costs since it has limited skilled nursing home care benefits. More extensive nursing home coverage is available through Medicaid but this program is only for individuals who have established financial need. Your parents should check with their attorney to learn how ownership of a house is treated under this program.

Paying their own way

No. 49 (on pages 155 and 156) discusses a long-term care insurance program that can protect assets for residents of some states; however, even if this insurance is available to or affordable by your parents, other ways to pay these costs should be reviewed.

Many parents of baby boomers are house rich and cash poor. How will they pay their own way for nursing home or other long-term care?

One option is to mine the value out of the family residence. It may be feasible for you or someone else to buy your parents' house and lease it back to them. Then, the purchase payments could pay for the needed care. Before taking this step, your parents should obtain legal and tax advice.

Another possibility is for your parents to take out a loan against their house. One potential problem with this approach is how the loan will be repaid.

A solution might be to have a loan known as a *reverse mortgage*. A reverse mortgage has the lending company paying the homeowner a certain amount each month (for *possibly* as long as the homeowner is alive) rather than the homeowner paying the lender each month (that's why it's called a reverse mortgage).

A reverse mortgage is very often used to provide additional income during retirement. With this type of loan, the homeowner is gambling that he or she will live long enough for the benefits of the monthly payments to outweigh the costs of the loan.

When is a reverse mortgage repaid? A reverse mortgage may require repayment when the homeowner dies, sells the house or enters a nursing home. If this third condition is part of the loan requirements, then this type of loan will not work to help pay for nursing home care.

A reverse mortgage needs to be reviewed carefully in advance by an attorney and qualified tax advisor because (1) it may give the lender the right to sell the house at a moment that is not beneficial for the family (e.g., when your parent enters the nursing home, the real estate market may be low) but is sufficient to pay the lender back, and (2) there is often a guaranteed fee for the lender (which is really additional interest) that could amount to hundreds of thousands of dollars even if the payments to your parents only last a short period of time. Before a reverse mortgage is taken out, the effect on all benefits should be considered.

Medigap insurance is not enough

Since Medicare does not cover all health expenses, there is usually a need for a supplemental health insurance policy commonly called a *Medigap* policy.

Although the name implies this type of policy is designed to fill in the gaps of Medicare coverage, there will probably still be a need for yet another policy to cover long-term care (including nursing home) costs. With health reform always around the corner, you'll need to keep up to date with developments concerning the coverage provided by various types of policies.

Long-term care insurance

In addition to a Medigap policy, your parents probably should have a *long-term care insurance policy*. Before your parents sign an application for such a policy, they should review with their attorney (1) the need for such a policy, (2) what alternatives are available, and (3) the terms and conditions of the policy.

Actually, you don't need to be elderly to buy and benefit from long-term care insurance. Younger people can use this coverage, too, if they suffer from heart attacks, strokes, cancer or even automobile accidents.

Age and health conditions may mean that your parents will not be eligible for this insurance. If your parents are eligible, see how their proposed (or current) policy covers the following items:

1. Alzheimer's disease should definitely be covered under the policy as well as Parkinson's disease. Check to see if any illnesses are not covered.

2. Pre-existing conditions should be covered (there will probably be a waiting period for such conditions—make sure the waiting period does not start anew each time a parent gets treated for the condition—otherwise the benefits may never be payable).

3. The policy benefits should be payable without having to first be hospitalized or in a skilled nursing facility before the nursing home stay or home care coverage begins.

4. The policy should be guaranteed renewable so it cannot be cancelled by the insurance company.

5. The premiums should be guaranteed to avoid increases if your parents' health worsens or as they get older (see if premiums are returned if your parents don't need the insurance benefits).

6. Review the maximum benefits during their lifetime as well as how they are calculated—per illness, per stay, a maximum dollar amount, a maximum number of days (look at competitive policies to get the best coverage).

7. Make sure the benefits can't be reduced.

8. Try to have an inflation protection option to increase the amount of benefits.

9. Check to see if your parents must live in a certain geographic area to receive the benefits under the policy in case your parents need to move (e.g., to be closer to you).

10. If there is a waiting period before benefits are payable, make sure your parents can afford to pay costs until the policy starts paying benefits.

11. See if the policy covers skilled nursing care, intermediate care, custodial care, and home health care (including funds to modify or remodel a home to accommodate changed circumstances and for a medical emergency communication system).

12. See if the policy covers adult day-care to allow your parents to live at home longer. Home day-care can provide a psychological benefit for your parents by allowing them to live at home and reduce the drain on their assets. Day-care costs are usually much less expensive than nursing home costs.

See if you can be named as a person to be notified if there's an unintentional lapse due to a failure of your parents to pay the insurance premium.

Make sure the insurance company is financially sound with a high rating from insurance ratings services such as A.M. Best, Moody's and Standard & Poor's. Each of these services describes their rating system as to what constitutes a high or low ranking. Ask your accountant about possible income tax benefits with these policies. Check with your attorney as to whether a policy without an income tax benefit offers better coverage.

Government assistance in paying for nursing home costs

Your parent(s) may need legal advice on eligibility requirements for long-term care at government expense.

Where to get legal advice

This is an area where the law keeps changing so it is important to have up-to-date information from an attorney who stays current on these matters. A possible source for an attorney is the National Academy of Elder Law Attorneys (1604 N. Country Club Road, Tucson AZ 85716, 1/520/881-4005).

49.

Nursing home insurance program may give special protection to your parents' assets

In 1993 Congress passed a law requiring states to attempt to recover nursing home costs from estates of deceased persons (including the estate of a surviving spouse) where those costs were paid by the government.

In connection with that law, a long-term care insurance policy (through assistance from the Robert Wood Johnson Foundation) was developed that could protect your parents' assets from the cost recovery program. At the time this book is being written, this insurance is only available in a few states (California, Connecticut, Indiana, and New York).

What is unique about this insurance is that it may allow someone to qualify for governmental aid and be exempt from state recovery efforts. That's because the policy does two things at once: (1) it reimburses the government for benefits given to your parents, and (2) it may exempt an equivalent amount of your parents' assets from these recovery efforts.

Thus, a person having some or even considerable assets could qualify for government assistance with nursing home costs and still protect one's assets.

This exemption will probably be available only up to the amount of this long-term care insurance that's actually purchased. Some states may be more liberal and exempt an unlimited amount of assets as long as a minimum size policy is purchased.

This insurance policy may protect assets, but not income, after the insurance benefits are exhausted. Also, not all of the costs of living and care will be paid by this type of insurance.

Your parents will need to review the insurance plans and eligibility requirements with their attorney.

This insurance is not available to everyone. Among the factors that may make one ineligible are pre-existing conditions and one's state of residency. And, not everyone will be able to afford this insurance.

LOOKING OUT
FOR YOUR PARENTS

50.

Telling your parents the financial facts of life before they remarry

In Nos. 35 through 39 on pages 123 through 129, you read about the many issues you face when you marry or remarry. These same issues apply to your parents, too, and there may even be another issue.

When our parents marry a new spouse, they very often want their assets to go to their children and original family.

Assuming the new couple (1) signs a marital agreement saying what's mine is mine and what's yours is yours, (2) signs new wills and/or trusts, (3) coordinates how title (ownership) on assets is set up so that it works with and not against the wills and trusts, and (4) signs any needed waivers on retirement plan benefits to allow children to benefit, there is still another issue for your parents to consider.

What will happen to the assets of *both* spouses if shortly after the remarriage, the senior citizen bride or groom needs long-term nursing home care? The expectation of the couple might be that the assets of the well spouse cannot be touched. Most people would imagine that once the assets of the ill spouse were exhausted, then governmental aid for nursing home costs could be obtained.

However, the law in your parent's state may delay governmental assistance until some or most of the assets of the well spouse are used to pay for nursing home costs (or the government might be able to make a claim against the assets of the well spouse after the death of the well spouse). Legal advice should be obtained to see how the law works in your parent's state.

This scenario may mean that this short remarriage results in depriving one of the ability to pass on an inheritance from a lifetime of work to one's children. Even worse, this is a case where saying "I do" can really mean "I'm elderly and could soon be broke."

Take a look at the strategies discussed in No. 48 and No. 49 on pages 149 through 156 to help protect your parent from this situation.

51.

Making sure your parents' health coverage doesn't expire at the border

Before your parents plan their next vacation, make sure their health coverage doesn't run out at the border.

Medicare provides limited coverage for medical services provided outside of the U.S. Make sure that any medical expenses incurred by your parents during a cruise or trip outside the U.S. are covered under a supplemental health insurance policy or under a travel insurance policy.

52.

The joint tenancy surprise: the down side of holding title as joint tenants

Joint tenancy (see also pages 123 and 137) means more than just a way to avoid probate in the event of a death. It can also have negative effects when parents and children hold ownership of assets together as joint tenants.

Financial risk of joint tenancy

If your parents put you and/or your brothers and sisters (or anyone else) on title as joint tenants on any of their assets, all of the joint tenants are co-owners of the jointly-owned assets (e.g., a house) while your parents are alive.

Besides gift tax, income tax, property tax, and death tax issues arising from joint tenancy, parents are taking a financial risk when they hold title as joint tenants with their children.

Although joint tenancy may afford more protection from creditors after the death of one of the joint tenants (see No. 44 on page 137), it can lead to more exposure to creditors while all the joint tenants are alive.

If, for example, one of your brothers or sisters has a business that goes under, then the creditors of that sibling may go after the sibling's portion of your parents' house while your parents are alive. If one of your siblings is at fault in a car accident where their car insurance is not enough to cover the damage, the injured party may also go after your sibling's portion of your parents' house while your parents are alive. In either of these examples the creditor could become a co-owner with your parents or possibly force a sale of the house (maybe even charge your parents rent for the interest in the house owned by the creditor).

So, if your parents want to avoid probate and also avoid being responsible for their children's debts and actions, they should talk to their attorney about setting up a *living trust* instead. A living trust is an arrangement that spells out who is to be the manager and beneficiary of assets while your parents are alive and after each of them passes away. A living trust, which is in essence a substitute for a will, allows successors to avoid the probate court after a death. (To be fully effective, however, certain asset transfers to the trust need to be done before a death.)

The bottom line is that while a technique such as joint tenancy may be good for one purpose (e.g., avoiding probate), it can have other, unintended, disastrous effects.

Also, if parents and children hold title as joint tenants and pass away simultaneously, such as in a car accident or a plane crash, the jointly held assets (e.g., a house, bank accounts, stocks, etc.) may go through several probates: the parents' and the children's. So, in such cases joint tenancy may not even give the benefit of avoiding probate.

Joint tenancy may disinherit intended beneficiaries

What do you think happens in this scenario: Your parents sign wills leaving everything equally to all of their four children, including you. They put one of your siblings on title to everything they own as a joint tenant. Both of your parents pass away. Who gets your parents' assets?

In general, it's going to be one person, the one sibling who was on title as a joint tenant.

A will or trust generally does not control assets held in joint tenancy. Unless an exception applies, assets held in joint tenancy pass outside of a will or trust to the surviving joint tenant.

In the above example, your parents probably wanted the one child to be able sign checks or take actions on their behalf if they became disabled. They probably did not want to give all of their assets to the one child.

Again, a living trust might be a safer way of dealing with disability or incompetency.

The bottom line is that you and your siblings should not have to face the joint tenancy surprise. Encourage your parents to see an attorney who can explain their options to them.

53.

The income tax surprise all siblings need to know

If your parents leave you and your sibling equal shares of their estate, you can accidentally wind up with less than your sibling. Your share may be the one that's subject to income tax.

Assume that your parents have two main assets (their house and their IRAs) and they are thinking of leaving them to their two children—you and your sibling.

If the house is worth about the same as the IRAs and you and your sibling don't get along well, your parents might think they were doing you a favor (and not harming either of you in any way) by leaving the house to your sibling and the IRAs to you. After all, this would avoid co-ownership and possibly fights between your sibling and you.

Your parents unfortunately made this decision before obtaining legal and tax advice so they weren't aware of the different consequences to you and your sibling. If your sibling inherits the house, it may never be subject to income tax. If you receive the IRAs, it *may* be income (depending upon the type of IRA and the holding period) to you and you may be paying income tax on all or a portion of the amount received. The solution is for your parents to get legal and tax advice so their estates are planned properly.

54.

The death tax surprise
all siblings need to know

Depending on how your parents' wills, trusts and beneficiary designations read, you may have the pleasure of paying death tax on assets inherited by your sibling.

Very often, wills and trusts stipulate that all the death taxes be paid from the "residue" of the estate covered by the documents.

Certain assets may pass automatically outside a will or trust upon a death such as joint tenancy assets and assets that have beneficiary designations (e.g., IRAs and life insurance).

Assume that your parents have two main assets (their house and their IRAs) and death tax will be due. In their wills they leave the house to you and they leave the IRAs under beneficiary designations to your sibling.

The wills might say death taxes on everything (including assets passing outside the will such as IRAs) will be paid from the assets (the house) covered by the will. This means that you would pay the death taxes on the house you inherited and on the IRAs *inherited by your sibling*. Is this what your parents intended? Again, make sure your parents get legal advice to properly plan their estates to avoid this tax result.

55.

Mentioning the unmentionable

We all have a reluctance to discuss terminal illness and death. Your parents should discuss both of these issues with the family and put their desires in writing. You should do the same to help your loved ones.

Terminal illness

There are two basic legal documents for handling a terminal illness: (1) a *health power of attorney* and (2) a *living will* (also sometimes called a *directive to physician* or *natural death declaration*).

A health power of attorney appoints an agent to make all the big and small health care decisions if one isn't able to speak for himself or herself. The biggest decision is whether to "pull the plug" (i.e., to be taken off life-support machines).

Your parents need to completely trust the agent they are naming. They should consider whether that person has any financial conflict of interest. For example, will the agent inherit from your parents if the plug is pulled? Often that's the case but that fact alone shouldn't rule a person out. Also, the agent should not have personal or religious beliefs that would prevent fulfillment of your parents' desired wishes.

The *living will* deals just with the big issue, pulling the plug. It's usually put into effect if there's an incurable and irreversible condition that has been diagnosed by two physicians and the condition either (1) will result in death within a relatively short time without the administration of life-sustaining treatment, or (2) has produced an irreversible coma or persistent vegetative state in which one is no longer able to make decisions regarding his or her medical treatment. Under such circumstances, a living will directs the attending physician to withhold or withdraw treatment that only prolongs an irreversible coma, a persistent vegetative state, or the process of dying. Such treatment is defined as "not necessary for your comfort or to alleviate pain" and could include the use of a respirator as well as artificially administered nutrition and hydration.

Spelling out funeral arrangements

If a will spells out funeral arrangements and is placed in a safe deposit box, it's possible no one may have access to the box until after the funeral is over.

Loved ones (and one's executor) should know in advance what is desired and also whether any arrangements have been made such as prepaid funeral or cremation costs.

Expressing desires in writing can avoid confusion or misunderstandings at a time when everyone is grieving.

A direction for funeral arrangements should cover at least the following items:

1. Nature of the desired ceremony (if any)—indicate whether it's to be religious or non-religious, elaborate or private
2. Name, address, phone number and title of the person to officiate and any special readings, passages or prayers to be included as part of the service
3. Name and location of ceremony and cemetery
4. Donation of body organs and directions regarding burial (headstone/monument requests) or cremation (disposition of ashes)
5. Any prepayments that have been made.

INSURING YOUR RETIREMENT

56.

The three questions you should ask about life insurance—before you buy

Before you buy life insurance, always ask yourself *and* your life insurance agent these three questions:

1. Why do I need this insurance?

2. What is the most this policy will cost me and for how many years under a worst-case scenario?

3. How much will I lose if I decide to cancel the policy early?

Do you need life insurance?

The first step in deciding whether to purchase life insurance is to determine your needs, which could include any of the following:

1. Making life more comfortable for a surviving spouse and/or children

2. Having enough money to raise and educate children in case of a death

3. Having a ready source of cash to pay death taxes so assets such as real estate or a family business won't have to be liquidated to meet tax obligations

4. Providing the funds to buy out the interest of a business partner if the partner dies

5. Paying for funeral costs and legal expenses upon a death

6. Building up a source of retirement income and assets.

If you have more than one need, then you may want more than one policy and/or more than one type of policy (for types of policies, see No. 57 on pages 176 to 179).

Not everyone, however, needs life insurance. For example, single persons with no dependents (i.e., no children or parents or other individuals dependent on them) may not need any life insurance other than to cover funeral costs.

Worst-case scenario

Before you purchase life insurance, you are usually handed a lengthy computer printout. On the printout are many columns with calculations explaining the cost and benefits of a policy.

This printout includes an optimistic projection (estimate) of your future costs and benefits. You also need to see in writing what the guaranteed result would be. In other words, what is the worst-case scenario as far as:

1. The number of years you will have to pay premiums

2. The amount of those premiums and how they might increase over the years

3. How low the benefits could drop.

Cost of dropping a policy early

Some insurance policies build up a "cash value" for you. You should find out what would be left of that cash value if you dropped a policy after 1, 5, 10, or 20 years.

57.

Buying the right amount and kind of life insurance

To determine the right amount and kind of life insurance you need, first analyze your purpose in buying the policy (see also No. 56 on pages 171 and 172).

For example, if the policy is to help pay for death taxes (see also No. 34 on pages 116 to 120 and No. 58 on page 180), you need to decide whether you are going to insure for the current value of your estate, a projected future value dependent upon your life expectancy and inflation rates, or something in between.

For a policy that is taken out to help support a spouse and/or children, you should go through the following four steps with your life insurance agent, financial advisor, and/or attorney to determine the right amount of life insurance.

Step one: calculate your net worth

This involves looking at what you have and what you owe. Be realistic in adding up your assets and subtracting your liabilities (the result is your *net worth*).

Savings accounts, life insurance, retirement plans, and stocks are assets that can provide ready cash for your estate. If you are married, calculate what will be available, including life insurance, in the event of (1) your death, (2) your spouse's death, and (3) both of your deaths. For other assets such as real estate (that your children won't be living in), estimate the sales price of your assets after you're gone.

As for your liabilities, identify when large payments on debts will be due. In particular, are there regular mortgage payments on your house or investment property that are spread out evenly over 15 or 30 years or is there a balloon (i.e., large) payment that's due next year or in five years?

Step two: add up death-related costs and expenses

To do this, subtract from your net worth the expected death tax, income tax, attorney's fees, executor's (or trustee's) fees, and other death-related costs (such as funeral expenses).

Step three: determine the future needs of your children and/or spouse

This entails looking at your children's (and possibly your spouse's) circumstances. How much you want to have on hand for small children can be a very different story compared to grown children who are financially comfortable on their own (a rarity these days, to be sure). Also, you may have one or more young or adult children who have special disabilities that require additional resources.

What standard of living do you want your spouse or children to have? Do you want your children to be able to attend private school as a youngster as well as a private college as an adult? What about money for their graduate studies, too?

Where will your young children be living if you're not a-round? Will the people you're naming as their guardians need to add on to their house to have your children live there, too? Are you able to provide for that?

*Step four: putting it all together to determine
your insurance requirements*

This step requires that you take all of the information from the first three steps and work backwards to come up with the necessary amount to leave for your children and/or spouse.

Begin by estimating the future income from your assets. Since we don't know what the future holds in the economy, you'll probably want to see results from different growth (e.g., 4%, 6%, 8%, and 10%) and inflation rates (e.g., 3%, 4%, 6%, and 8%).

Next, you should estimate how much your spouse and children will need per year (such as $10,000 for one child and $15,000 for another child) and build in an inflation factor for these expenses, too. Consider how much your family will be receiving from Social Security for survivors benefits.

Once you calculate the expected income and expenses over the years, you'll be able to see how long your money will last. Will your money be gone before all of your children are age 21? Age 18? Age 12?

The last decision is whether you want some money left over to give to your children after they attain a certain age (for example, age 21).

Use these four steps and make any necessary adjustments to calculate the sum of money you'll need to have on hand to provide for your family. A rule of thumb is to insure for five to eight times your annual salary in taking care of young children. If you have many children and just two thumbs, this rule may be too expensive to follow.

Do you want the IRS as a beneficiary on your life insurance?

You should remember that some of the insurance proceeds may go to the IRS instead of to your family, depending upon the size of your estate and the way you own life insurance. Talk to your attorney (and see No. 58 on page 180) about ways to insure that life insurance passes to your family free of federal death tax.

Types of policies and uses

Once you decide how much life insurance you need, the next step is to decide on the right kind of insurance for you.

There are two main types of life insurance: *cash value* and *term*. There are variations of each type of policy and some policies combine both types of insurance within one policy package.

Term insurance

Term insurance is the easier one to understand. Term insurance is like renting insurance—as long as you pay your premium, a death benefit will be paid. You don't own anything with term insurance. If you stop paying the premium, you walk away with nothing and no death benefit is payable.

If you are getting term insurance, purchase an annual renewable term policy so you don't have to pass physical exams each year to keep the policy as long as you want it.

Term insurance is more appropriate for shorter-term needs. For example, if you have children who are college-age or younger, you might want to be sure that there is enough money to educate them or to provide for them to age 18 or 21.

One mistake that is often made in families where both spouses work is the assumption that the kids will be able to get by, if they have to, on the income of one spouse. Well, what happens to that theory if both spouses pass away in a car accident? It's no fun thinking about the terrible possibilities that are out there, but part of the responsibility of being a parent is to make sure children are provided for in any eventuality. So, consider insuring each spouse.

Term insurance premium costs are initially lower than cash value life insurance but they may increase rapidly as one gets older (since the risk of dying increases over time, too).

You can have term insurance and at the same time keep premiums at the same level rate by purchasing *level premium term insurance*. With this type of insurance, the premium stays at the same cost for a specified period of time, such as 10 years, 15 years, or 20 years.

Since cost is a factor, always determine the cost of term insurance (including level term insurance) before making your decision.

Cash value life insurance

Cash value life insurance is a combination of term insurance (it provides a death benefit) with a tax-deferred investment component.

Cash value life insurance is generally intended to be lifelong insurance (rather than for a shorter term) and it costs more than term insurance in the earlier years.

There are many variations of cash value life insurance. They range from conservative to more risky in their operation and effect. In general, all types of cash value life policies allow for tax-deferred growth and non-taxable distributions through loans and withdrawals.

The oldest type is *traditional whole life insurance*. There are more guarantees on the ultimate premiums and benefits with this type of cash value life insurance. One use is as a source to pay death taxes.

A variation on traditional whole life insurance that has greater risk (and possibly greater rewards or losses) is *universal* (or *flexible* or *adjustable*) *life insurance*. With this type of insurance, a policyholder gets some flexibility in the amount of premium that needs to be paid each year and the amount of life insurance in place at any given time. Younger people with changing needs and the willingness to take risks often look to this type of policy.

Another variation is called *variable insurance*. It is similar to traditional whole life or universal life insurance but the investment component is very often put in mutual funds. It's the riskiest because if the investments do not work out, you can lose not only your cash value in the policy *but also* your coverage as well. However, if the investments do work out, you can reduce the size of your premium payments.

The potential candidates for this type of insurance are usually persons who need life insurance and have fully utilized the other tax-deferral vehicles such as retirement plans (including IRAs, 401(k) plans, and Keogh plans). Again, younger people with changing needs and the willingness to take risks often look to this type of policy.

Special life insurance for married couples

Spouses can also purchase permanent insurance that pays either (1) on the first death or (2) on the second death of two insureds.

The first type of policy, often called *first-to-die insurance*, can be used for a family where both spouses work and the survivor would need insurance to replace the income of the spouse who died.

The second type of policy, often called *second-to-die insurance,* is commonly used to replenish an estate for death taxes that will be due on the death of the second spouse. This type of policy is generally less expensive than two separate policies because it is covering the lives of two people but the insurance company is paying off only one time, and only after two insureds have passed away. See page 180 on ways to eliminate death tax on life insurance.

Get a sound company

As with any insurance, make sure the insurance company is rated highly by A.M. Best, Moody's, Standard & Poor's, Weiss Research and Duff & Phelps.

You could reduce your risk on any sizeable amount of insurance by using two companies rather than one. You'll need to compare any extra cost with the comfort you'll receive splitting the coverage between two companies.

Since life insurance is a long-term investment, you'll need a well established and financially sound company when the time comes to collect proceeds.

58.

Ways to avoid
death tax on life insurance

In general, each person can bequeath up to $625,000 (the *federal death tax exemption* limit) in 1998 with no federal death tax (U.S. citizen spouses can leave an unlimited amount to each other with no death tax until both spouses are gone). By the year 2006, the $625,000 figure will reach $1,000,000.

Most people think you don't count life insurance when you are determining whether federal death tax is due. Actually, it depends. If life insurance pushes you over the federal death tax exemption limit (or if you're already above that amount), your estate could land in the taxing zone, a zone that starts at least the 37% rate and goes up from there.

What this means is that a good portion or even a majority of the insurance policy proceeds on your death could go to *Uncle Sam* rather than to your real family. If you don't do advance planning, you might as well name Uncle Sam on the beneficiary designation form.

There are two ways, however, to keep the insurance proceeds from being taxable for death tax purposes: either have an *irrevocable life insurance trust* (i.e., a trust that cannot be changed) or have your children own, apply for, and pay for the policy.

Ask your attorney whether a life insurance trust or direct ownership (and premium payments) by your children makes sense for you. The time to ask about all of this is before you apply for a policy although certain steps can be taken to utilize existing policies, too.

59.

The right and wrong way
to name beneficiaries

Beneficiary designations generally override your will or trust.

If the beneficiaries under your will or trust differ from those selected in other designations (e.g., life insurance, retirement plan, and IRA), you should make it clear in your will or trust that this has been done intentionally. This will avoid potentially costly fights and help keep family harmony. Also, consider the income tax and death tax ramifications resulting from beneficiary designations (see No. 53 and No. 54 on pages 165 and 166).

Three overlooked issues in beneficiary designations

The first issue involves the consequences of failing to specify a secondary or contingent beneficiary on a beneficiary form. If your primary beneficiary does not survive you, that can mean in many cases that the benefits will be paid to your estate.

There are two main problems with benefits going into your estate. First, the benefits become subject to attorney's and executor's fees and delays that might otherwise have been avoided. Second, if the benefits are paid to your estate, an asset that may have been exempt from creditors' claims might well be converted to one that could be taken by creditors.

The second overlooked issue in beneficiary designations involves failing to specify what will happen to the benefits earmarked for a child if the child does not outlive you but leaves a child (your grandchild) who does survive you. Your beneficiary designation can be worded to deal with this possibility.

The third issue concerns whether you've named individual(s) or a trust on your beneficiary designation. Whom you name as beneficiaries can determine how long income tax may be postponed on certain retirement benefits. Your attorney and tax advisor can tell whether this tax postponement possibility is available to you.

Keep designations current

Always keep your beneficiary designations up to date to reflect your current intent and do so with the assistance of legal advice to make sure the designation works with, and not against, your estate plan.

60.

What to look for in a disability insurance policy

Disability policies are not all the same. They can vary widely in cost and benefits. In general, there are two benefits from purchasing a policy while you are younger: (1) the cost is lower and (2) you are still insurable and not subject to a health condition that may disqualify you from coverage.

When you find a policy, see how it handles at least the following seven items:

1. Check if the benefits are payable for life (or at least until age 65) instead of a maximum period such as for five years. Keep in mind that normal retirement age for baby boomers is between age 66 and 67—it's not age 65.

2. See if the benefits *(a)* increase with inflation (i.e., is there a "cost-of-living adjustment" or "COLA"?) or *(b)* give you options to increase coverage over time without the requirement of a physical examination rather than just staying a fixed dollar amount during the life of the policy.

3. Review the definition of the term *disability* in the policy to see if benefits will be paid if you can't work in your *current occupation* or only if you can't do *any kind of work.*

4. Calculate how long you can afford to wait before the benefits become payable—one month, three months, one year. The longer the waiting period, the lower the premium. Don't be overly optimistic about your ability

to survive financially while you are disabled. A three-month waiting period might be realistic for you.

5. Since partial disabilities are not uncommon, check to see if partial disability benefits are included without your having to be totally disabled.

6. See whether premiums are waived (excused) if you are disabled.

7. Read the policy to be sure you understand the exclusions under the policy.

Finally, see if your policy can be converted into a long-term care policy at retirement age irrespective of your medical condition is at that time.

Who should pay the premiums?

If you become disabled and receive benefits under a disability insurance policy, those benefits may or may not be free of income tax. Having income-tax free benefits could be extremely important to you while you are disabled.

In general, if you personally pay the insurance premiums as compared to a company paying the premiums, the benefits will be income-tax free to you. If, instead, your employer pays the premiums, then the benefits will be subject to income tax. Be sure to review this topic with your disability insurance agent, accountant, and attorney.

TAKING CARE OF BUSINESS

61.

Three steps every business owner has to consider

Nearly 90% of U.S. businesses are family businesses. You may be a part or sole owner of such a business. Since fewer than one in three family businesses survives into the second generation, you may need to deal with a few family business facts of life.

Every business owner needs to consider taking the following three steps:

1. Sign a written agreement dealing with future ownership of the business.

   Are you involved in a family business with one or both of your parents? Your siblings? Your children? You probably need a written agreement covering the succession of ownership in the event of death or disability.

   Will one or more of your children want to sell their shares to outsiders without giving the other children a chance to match any outside offer? Will you want to restrict their ability to do so with a written agreement?

2. Have a will or trust that considers family involvement or non-involvement of children in the business.

   Are only some of your children working in the family business? If you passed away, you might want *only* the children working in the business to inherit it from you.

If you left the business to all the children, it might create problems for them. The "non-working children" might want larger non-deductible dividends paid to them rather than the reinvestment of profits into the business. The working children might try to have the business pay them exorbitant salaries to reduce the profits paid out to the non-working children.

If possible, you might want to leave the business only to the children working in the business. The other children would then receive other assets. If you don't have other assets comparable in value to the business, you might want to use life insurance to equalize the amount of assets passing to all of your children.

3. Plan in advance the sources to pay death taxes.

Death taxes may force the business to be sold no matter what agreement has been signed. Instead, life insurance could provide the funds to pay death taxes so the operation of the business could continue unaffected. See No. 58 on page 180 for ways to avoid death tax on the life insurance proceeds.

An agreement for succession of ownership of the business as well as coordinated wills, trusts, and life insurance policies can produce a smooth and equitable result for all of your family.

62.

What you need to know if you have a partner in real estate or business

If you have a partner in real estate or business, you need to prepare yourself for what the future may hold for your partnership with respect to your estate planning.

Depending upon how you hold title (ownership) with your partner, the partner may receive those assets upon your death.

That's because you may hold title in a way that overrides your will or trust so that your share automatically passes to your partner. You should have your attorney check title to your assets so that your intended beneficiaries receive your assets upon your death.

To add insult to injury, it's possible that unless you take steps to prevent it, your loved ones would have to pay death taxes on assets going to your partner.

You might also want to have a written agreement with your partner giving you an option to buy out your partner's interest in the business or real estate if your partner dies, becomes disabled, or just wants to sell his or her interest. Otherwise, you might end up co-owning the real estate or business with strangers or your partner's children.

MAKING MONEY FROM YOUR PAPERWORK

63.

How financial records can save you taxes on your house

Having organized financial records can save you income taxes when you sell your house. Too many people are going to make a mistake and stop keeping track of home improvements thinking the $250,000/$500,000 federal exclusions under the 1997 tax act will eliminate the need to keep records.

Selling your house

You may owe income tax when you sell your house.

When you sell your house, income tax may be due on the gain above your original cost plus improvements. You need to have organized records to keep track of the improvements that may reduce the income tax due on a sale. You should set up a separate file that makes it easy to store and locate the invoices and checks to substantiate the improvements made to your house.

Although there are ways to avoid paying federal income tax if you sell your house, at some point you may have to pay the piper. (See No. 21 on pages 73 and 74 on how the gain may not be taxed at all.)

There are three reasons to still keep track of improvements even with the 1997 federal law. First, the new tax law is a federal law, not a state law. Your state may have different rules. Even if your state adopts a law just like the federal law, you may move to a new state (or to a vacation home there) that has different rules. Second, there may be great inflation in the coming years so that the $250,000/$500,000 exclusions will not cover the gain over the coming decades. Third, the federal income tax rules may change over time.

64.

How financial records can save you taxes on stocks and mutual funds

If you invest in stocks or mutual funds, from time to time you'll want or need to sell shares to buy a house, pay for your children's college education, or take a needed vacation.

Stocks or mutual funds may be in a tax-deferred investment (e.g., a traditional IRA) that will grow income-tax free (including gains on sale) until distributions are taken out.

However, you may own such stocks or funds just in your own name and sales would be subject to income tax. You may be able to reduce or eliminate the income tax on such a sale of stock or mutual fund share if you have organized records.

If an investment has gone up in value since you purchased it, you will owe income tax on the sale of that investment. Very often you will have purchased additional shares over time. Will you owe income tax if some of the investment has gone up and some has gone down in value since you purchased it?

With organized records, you could direct the sale of those portions of your stock or mutual fund shares that produced the lowest income tax due.

How to avoid paying extra, unnecessary income tax

If you invest in a mutual fund and reinvest the dividends rather than take them out, organized records may allow you to reduce the gain upon a sale.

Suppose you put $1,000 into a fund in your personal name (and outside of any retirement plan or IRA) and over the years you received $300 in dividends, which were reinvested in the fund. You now have $1,300 invested. When you decide to sell your interest in the fund for $2,000, good records will show that you have $700 of gain ($2,000 less $1,300) not $1,000 of gain ($2,000 less $1,000) since the reinvested dividends were previously taxed.

Tracking down your stock cost basis

You may need assistance in figuring out how much you've paid for stock that you bought over time or through payroll deductions. The first place to look is your library and see if the Standard and Poor's Guide gives you enough information. If not, you might want to contact Prudential American Securities (1/626/795-5831, California) and for a fee they'll search for information you can use to reconstruct your purchase history.

65.

Finding lost treasures

Hundreds of billions of dollars in assets have been misplaced in the United States. This money is being held by the federal government, state government, insurance companies and banks. It's not surprising considering the way people move around the country, change their names, change their jobs, forget to send in change of address forms and fall prey to a fading memory as the years go by. Add to that the frenzied pace of company mergers and corporate name changes and you have a recipe for lost treasure.

Fortunately, it's getting easier to track down lost assets. A good starting point is the National Association of Unclaimed Property Administrators. You can go to their Website (http://www.intersurf.com/~naupa/). You can also check out lists put out by states on their Internet sites. When in doubt, check everywhere including life insurance companies and government pension plans. Old checkbook registers and income tax returns are good sources to help locate lost assets.

U.S. Savings Bonds

Too many people do not keep track of their U.S. Savings Bonds maturity dates. Bonds don't pay interest forever so don't let yours be among those that have stopped earning interest. Also see page 101 for resource information on Savings Bonds.

Finding vital records

If you need to locate a certified copy of a birth, death, marriage or divorce certificate, get a copy of the U.S. Department of Health and Human Services' booklet "Where to Write for Vital Records."

You can order the booklet by calling 1/719/948-4000 or see it on-line at http://www.pueblo.gsa.gov/misc.htm.

APPENDIX

Appendix

Examples of Social Security Retirement, Disability and Survivors benefits

Retirement benefit examples

For these examples of monthly Social Security retirement benefits, assume you and your spouse were age 45 in 1997, you have had steady lifetime earnings and retire at full retirement age rather than taking an early retirement:

Your 1996 earnings	Your monthly benefit	Monthly benefit for you and your spouse (See Note 1 below)
$20,000	$ 797	$1,195
30,000	1,063	1,594
40,000	1,229	1,843
50,000	1,354	2,031
62,700	1,519	2,278

or more (See Note 2 below)

The accuracy of these estimates depends on the pattern of your actual past earnings and on your earnings in the future.

Note 1: Your spouse is assumed to be the same age as you. Your spouse may qualify for a higher retirement benefit based on his or her own work record.

Note 2: Assumes earnings were equal to or greater than the OASDI wage base from age 22 through 1996.

Disability benefit examples

For these examples of monthly Social Security disability benefits, assume you were age 45 in 1997, became disabled in 1997 and had steady lifetime earnings (the following survivors benefit examples assume you passed away in 1997):

Your 1996 earnings	Your monthly benefit	Monthly benefit for you, your spouse, and child
$20,000	$ 797	$1,195
30,000	1,063	1,595
40,000	1,229	1,844
50,000	1,348	2,023
62,700	1,445	2,168
or more (See Note 2 above)		

The accuracy of these estimates and the survivors benefits below depends on the pattern of your earnings in prior years.

Survivors benefit examples

Your 1996 earnings	Monthly benefit for your spouse and one child	Monthly benefit for your spouse and two children
$20,000	$1,194	$1,459
30,000	1,594	1,874
40,000	1,844	2,152
50,000	2,030	2,370
62,700	2,184	2,549
or more (See Note 2 above)		

Great Way to Search the Internet

If you want to minimize frustration in searching the Internet for information, check out *Inference Find.*

The best way I've found to locate information, Web sites or resources is *Inference Find* (http://www.inference.com/ifind/).

Inference Find is a fast Internet search tool that combines the results of many search engines and groups the results in understandable categories. Just call up the site, type in your search request and seven seconds later, you can view the organized results on your screen.

Software and Internet Sites of Interest

Software to do retirement planning

Before you purchase software to do retirement planning, please check whether (1) the software has been updated for the latest federal tax legislation, (2) you're purchasing the latest version of the program and (3) your computer has enough power and speed to make using the program enjoyable and rewarding.

You might want to purchase both of the programs listed below and do your retirement calculations with each program. When you order, check on the current product name, features and computer requirements. You can also do calculations on-line on some of the Internet sites listed on pages 204 and 205.

- *Vanguard Retirement Planner*

  Call 1/800/876-1840. The program is inexpensive, easy to use and uses graphics very effectively.

- *Quicken Deluxe for Windows (by Intuit)*

  Call 1/800/224-0991. You should also ask about another software product, the *Financial Planner.*

On-line financial information (Web site addresses do change.)

AARP
http://www.aarp.org

College cost calculations and sources of financial aid
http://finaid.org/
http://www.vanguard.com

Education about basic investment information:
http://www.aaii.org

Financial information
http://www.americanexpress.com/direct
http://www.cnnfn.com/quickenonfn/
http://www.smartmoney.com

Internal Revenue Service
http://www.irs.gov

IRA calculations: Roth IRA vs. traditional IRA
Vanguard IRA Worksheet on their Internet Web site
(http://www.vanguard.com)

Mortgage loans
http://QuickenMortgage.com

Pension benefits
http://www.dol.gov/dol/pwba/welcome.html

Retirement planning
http://www.americanexpress.com/direct (select Financial
        Tools, then select Retirement Savings)
http://quicken.excite.com (under Retirement, select Getting
        Started and then select Build Your Plan)
http://www.fidelity.com (select Personal Investing, then select
        Retirement Investing, then select Retirement
        Toolkit and then select Retirement Planning
        Calculator)
http://www.vanguard.com (select Planning Center, then
        select Retirement Resource Center, then select
        Planning for Retirement, then select How Much
        Should You Save for Retirement)

Social Security
http://www.ssa.gov

Books Worth Considering

The Privacy Rights Handbook: How To Take Control of Your Personal Information by Beth Givens and The Privacy Rights Clearinghouse (Avon Books).

"It's vital to get *The Privacy Rights Handbook* to the millions of Americans who are unaware of how 'invisible hands' manipulate their daily life."
— Ralph Nader (from the Foreword)

The book is available in bookstores or it may be purchased directly from the Privacy Rights Clearinghouse (1/619/298-3396, California).

A Parent's (and Grandparent's) Guide to Wills & Trusts by Don Silver (Adams-Hall Publishing).

"Excellent book. It is clear. It is concise. It is clever."
— *Los Angeles Times*

The book is available in bookstores or it may be purchased directly from Adams-Hall Publishing (1/800/888-4452, California).

Index

A

AARP, 82, 204
  Web site, 204
Accelerated death benefit, 91
Accountant
  advice from, 9, 22, 25-26, 28,
    29, 43, 46-48, 50, 53, 54,
    55, 57, 58, 59, 62, 65, 67,
    73-74, 103, 103, 108, 110,
    133, 144-146, 153, 165, 173,
    182, 184, 193-194
  financial planner
    recommended by, 31
  sale of residence and, 60, 73-
    74, 193-194
Adjustable life insurance. *See* Life
  insurance
Alternative minimum tax, 58
Alzheimer's disease. *See also*
  Incapacity
  long-term care insurance and,
    152
American Express
  Web site, 205
American Express CreditAware,
  96
AmeriCorps, 109
Annuities, 63-68
  companies issuing, 65
  definition of, 63
  duration of, 65
  fees and early withdrawals of,
    30, 59
  financial strength of
    companies issuing, 65
  fixed-rate, 66-67
  flexible, 66

IRAs compared to, 67-68
  mutual funds and, 67-68
  need for, 64-65
  nest egg compared to, 63-64
  retirement plan payouts and,
    134
  Roth IRA and, 68
  single-premium, 66
  surrender costs of, 59
  variable, 59, 67-68
  withdrawals from, 28, 30, 59,
    66-68
Ante-nuptial agreements. *See*
  Marital agreement
Assumptions
  retirement planning, 39-45
  Social Security, 201-202

B

Bankruptcy
  retirement plans and, 134
B trust. *See* Death tax
Beneficiary designations
  creditors and, 134, 181
  death tax and, 166, 176,
    180
  gaps and, 135, 181-182
  income tax and, 165, 182
  irrevocable life insurance trusts
    and, 180
  marriage and, 125, 128-129
  naming of beneficiaries and,
    181-182
  remarriage and, 125, 182

Beneficiary designations
(continued)
saving taxes and, 62
waivers and, 159
Blended families, 99, 101, 141, 144
Bonds, U.S. Savings, 47, 101, 104,
197
Books
*A Parent's Guide to Wills &
Trusts*, 206
The Privacy Rights Handbook,
95, 206
Budget, 21, 23
Business
agreement as to, 187-189
death taxes and, 188-189
life insurance and, 171, 180,
188
ownership of, 187-189
partnership, 187-189
wills and trusts and, 187-189

C

Calculations
college education, 112-115
Web sites, 204, 205
life insurance, 173-179, 188
retirement, 36-45, 204-205
California, long-term care
insurance in, 151-156
Capital gain tax, 10, 57-60
alternative minimum tax and,
58
saving taxes, 26, 28-30, 51, 57-
60, 68, 102-104, 193-196
selling residence and, 58-59,
73-74, 193-194
Cash value life insurance, 177-179
Certified Public Accountant. *See*
Accountant
Children. *See also* College
education
beneficiary designations and,
181-182

business and, 187-189
death taxes and, 128, 166, 178-
179, 180, 188
family business and, 187-189
homeschooling and, 87-89
housing and, 84-85
income tax on inheritance to,
165
joint tenancy and, 162-164
life insurance and, 171, 173-
179, 188
marriage and, 128-129, 159-160
nursing home costs and
inheritance for, 159-160
partnership and, 187, 189
protecting inheritance for,
128-129, 187-189
reducing death tax for, 116-
120, 180
remarriage and, 128-129, 159-
160
Social Security benefits and,
11-12
trust and, 128-129, 187-189
will and, 128-129, 187-189
CNNfn
Web site, 205
COLA, 183
College education
advanced placement classes
and, 110-111
blended families and, 101
community college and, 109
credit report and, 96
financial aid and effect of
savings on, 100-109
Web site, 204-205
gifts for, 105-107, 110-111
government service and, 109
grandparents as source for,
105, 111
home equity loans and, 110
Hope credits and, 106-107

College education (continued)
how much to save for, 112-115
Web site, 204
IRAs and, 105-107
junior college and, 109
Kiddie Tax and, 102-104
life insurance and, 108-109, 171, 173-179
marriage and, 124, 126
National Association of Student Financial Aid Administrators, 110
piggy bank saving technique for, 19
record keeping and, 195-196
saving for, 19, 100, 112-115
sources to pay for, 100-111, 171, 173-179
term insurance and, 176-177
trusts and saving for, 103
tuition prepayment plans for, 108
UGMA and, 102
U.S. Savings Bonds and saving for, 101
UTMA and, 102
Web site, 204
zero-coupon bonds and, 110
Comfortable retirement
amount of income for, 34-35, 39-45
examples of savings requirements for, 36-38, 39-45
Community college, 109
Company retirement plan
checking benefits of, 15-18
death taxes and, 166
errors in, 15-16
income tax on inheritance of, 165
IRA rollover of, 55, 61-62
rollovers of, 55, 61-62
summary plan description of, 16-17, 62
withdrawals from, 55, 61-62
Compound growth, 24, 26, 35
Compound interest, 24, 35, 38, 72
Conduit IRA, 50
Connecticut, long-term care insurance in, 155-156
Conservator, 92-93
Conservatorship, 92-93
Cost-of-living adjustment, 183
CPA/Financial Specialist, 33
CreditAware, 96
Credit cards, 21-22
Creditors
accelerated death benefit and, 91
bankruptcy and, 134
beneficiary designations and, 181
Robert Wood Johnson Foundation, 155-156
joint tenancy and, 137, 162-164
life insurance and, 91, 135
living trust and, 137-138
long-term care insurance and, 149-156
marriage and, 159-160
nursing home costs and, 149-156
parents' medical costs while traveling and, 161
remarriage and, 159-160
retirement plan assets and, 134
trusts and, 137-138
umbrella insurance and, 136
Credit reports, 95-96, 206
Credits. See Tax credits.
Credit shelter trust. See Death tax
Cruise America, 83

D

Death. See Funeral arrangements

Death tax
  amount of inheritance and, 30,
    42, 116, 165, 166, 175-176,
    180, 188, 189
  B Trust and, 117
  business and, 187-189
  children and, 128-129, 175,
    180, 187-189
  college education fund, effect
    on, 100
  credit shelter trust and, 117
  death-tax saving trust and,
    117
  exemption amount, 116-117
  exemption trust, 117
  family business and, 187-189
  IRAs and, 58, 166
  irrevocable trusts and, 180
  life insurance and, 135, 176,
    178, 179, 180
  marital deduction, 118, 124,
    128-129
  married couple's exempt
    amount, 116-117
  moving and effect on, 145
  QTIP trust, 124, 128-129
  qualified terminable interest
    trust, 124, 128-129
  retirement plans and, 58, 166
  second-to-die life insurance
    and, 179
  state inheritance tax, 118
Death tax saving trust. *See* Death
  tax
Debt. *See* Credit cards; Mortgage
Defined benefit plans, 15, 16
Directive to physician. *See* Living
  will
Disability. *See* Incapacity
Disability benefits
  part-time work and, 86-88
  Social Security as source of,
    11-12, 86-88, 202
Disability insurance, 183-184

Disinheritance
  joint tenancy and, 162-164
Distributions from retirement
  plans. *See* Retirement plans
Diversify investments, 27, 47, 50,
  81
Divorce, 123
  effect on college education
    fund, 101
  real estate and, 74
  Social Security benefits affected
    by, 13, 127
Domicile, 145

E

Early withdrawals. *See*
  Retirement plans
Economy
  predicting, 40-41,
Education IRA, 53, 105-106
Education savings
  piggy bank technique for, 19
El Monte RV, 83
Equifax, 96
Errors
  company retirement plans
    and, 15-17
  Social Security benefits and,
    12-14
Ethical wills, 79-80
Exemption Trust. *See* Death tax
Experian, 96

F

Family business. *See* Business
FDIC, 52
Federal Deposit Insurance
  Corporation. *See* FDIC
Fidelity
  Web site, 205
Financial advisor
  Certified Financial Planner, 32
  CFP, 32

Financial advisor (continued)
  Chartered Financial
    Consultant,33
  ChFC, 33
  CPA/Personal Financial
    Specialist, 33
  factors in selecting, 31-33
  meeting your objectives, 33
  qualifications of, 31-33
  questions to ask a, 31-32
  questions to be asked by, 32
  selecting, 31-33
First-to-die insurance, 178-179
Fixed-rate annuity. See Annuities
Flexible annuity. See Annuities
Flexible life insurance, 178. See
    also Life insurance
401(k) plan
  beneficiary designations and,
    181-182
  benefits and, 20, 27, 49
  conduit IRA and, 50
  dangers in borrowing against,
    49, 50
  death tax and, 166
  features of, 15, 20, 49-51, 64
  FDIC insurance limitations, 52
  income tax on inheritance of,
    165
  reducing taxes and, 28-30, 49,
    50, 56
  Roth IRA and, 49
403(b) plan, 75
457 plan, 75
Franklin, Ben, 21, 87
Funeral arrangements, 168

G

Gifts
  for college education, 105-107,
    110-111, 119
  for housing, 84-85
  for medical bills, 119

  grandparents and college
    education, 105, 111
  irrevocable trusts and, 180
  life insurance and, 91, 119-120
  reducing death tax with, 119
Gift tax exclusion, 111
Good Sam Club, 83
GoRVing Coalition, 83
Government retirement plans, 75
Grandchildren. See Children
Granny houses, 84-85
Guardianship, 92-94, 124, 174

H

Health matters, 34, 35, 76, 90, 91,
  92-94, 145, 149-156, 159-160,
  161. See also Medical costs
Health power of attorney, 92-94,
  167-168
Home equity loan
  dangers and, 22
  deducting interest and, 22
Home offices, 84-85, 87, 89
Homeschooling, 87-89
Hope Credits, 106-107
House. See Real estate

I

Illiquid investments
  family business as, 187-188
  partnership, 189
  real estate, 70, 174, 189
Incapacity
  conservator and, 92-94
  conservatorship and, 92-94
  disability insurance and, 183-
    184
  health power of attorney and,
    92-94, 167-168
  living trusts and, 92-94, 162-
    164
  living will and, 92-94, 167-168

Incapacity (continued)
  long-term care insurance and,
    149-156
  money power of attorney and,
    92-94
  Social Security benefits and,
    202
  work as preventative of, 90
Income tax. *See also* Capital gain
    tax
  beneficiary designations and,
    182
  cash value life insurance and,
    177-78
  deducting interest and, 22, 146
  disability insurance and, 183-
    184
  Hope Credits, 106-107
  inheritance of IRAs and, 165,
    182
  inheritance of retirement plans
    and, 165
  IRA, 9-10, 53-55, 165
  IRS Web site, 205
  Kiddie Tax and, 102-104
  life insurance and, 91, 177-178
  Medical Savings Account and,
    76
  moving and, 144
  MSA and, 76
  mutual funds and, 10, 195-196
  ordinary income tax. *See*
    Capital gains tax
  purchase of residence and,
    146, 193-194
  refinancing and, 133, 146
  Roth IRA, 9-10, 53-55, 68
  second income, net of, 86-89
  selling residence and, 73-74,
    193-194
  stay-at-home parent and, 86-
    89
  stepped-up basis and, 10, 58-
    59
  stocks and, 10, 28, 51, 195-196

  title and, 123
  ways to reduce, 9-10, 28-30,
    51, 53-55, 56-60, 102-104,
    193-194, 195-196
Indiana, long-term care insurance
  in, 155-156
Individual retirement account. *See*
  IRA
Inference Find, 203
Inflation
  bonds, 47
  college education and, 112-115
  considering effects of, 27, 35,
    36, 39, 40-41, 43, 47, 194
  life insurance amount and,
    173-179
  long-term care insurance and,
    152
  real bonds and, 47
Inheritance
  business and, 187-189
  death taxes, effect on, 43, 166,
    187-189
  effect on size of nest egg, 39-
    45
  family business and, 187-189
  income tax and, 165
  joint tenancy and, 162-164
  life insurance and, 171
  marriage and, 159-60
  nursing home costs and, 159-
    160
  partnership and, 189
  remarriage and, 159-160
  stepped-up income tax basis
    and, 10, 58-59
Inheritance tax. *See* Death tax
Insurance. *See also* Disability
    insurance
  Robert Wood Johnson
    Foundation and, 155-156
  life insurance
    financial strength of
    companies issuing, 65, 179
  long-term care, 149-156

Insurance (continued)
  Medicare limitations while
    traveling and, 161
  nursing home cost, 149-156
Interest
  credit cards and, 21-22
  401(k) plan loan and, 49-50
  home equity loan and, 22
  mortgage and, 22, 69-72
  purchasing residence and, 146
  refinancing and, 133, 146
Internet. *See* Web sites.
  searching of, 203, 204-205
Intuit, see Quicken
Investments
  monitoring of, 27
  right, 46-48, 50, 51
IRA
  annuities, compared to, 66-68
  beneficiary designations and,
    181-182
  children establishing, 104
  conduit, 50
  death tax and, 166
  distributions from, 9-10, 105-
    106, 182
  early withdrawals from, 61-62
  Education IRA, 100, 105-106
  income tax on inheritance
    and, 165
  inheritance of, 165
  limitation on FDIC insurance
    for, 52
  rollovers to, 50, 55, 61-62
  Roth IRA, 9-10, 24-26, 49, 53-
    55, 68, 106, 107
  withdrawals and, 28-30, 68
Irrevocable trusts, 137-138
  life insurance and, 180

J

Johnson, Robert Wood Foundation
  nursing home insurance and,
    155-156

Joint tenancy
  business and, 189
  creditors and, 137, 162-164
  disinheritance and, 162-164
  inheritance and, 162-164
  living trusts as compared to,
    162-164
  marriage and, 123-124
  partnership and, 189
  probate and, 163
Junior college, 109

K

Keogh
  beneficiary designations and,
    181-182
  income tax on inheritance of,
    165
  limitation on FDIC insurance,
    52
Kiddie Tax
  college education and, 102-104

L

Level-premium term insurance,
  177
Liability
  death tax and, 166, 180
  income tax on inheritance,
    165, 182
  joint tenancy and, 162-164
  mortgage due date, 174
  refinancing and, 133
  retirement plans and, 134, 181-
    182
Liens
  nursing home costs and, 155-
    156
Life expectancy. *See* Life span
Life insurance
  accelerated death benefits and,
    91

Life insurance (continued)
adjustable, 178
beneficiary designations and,
181-182
both spouses working and,
177-179
businesses and, 188
cash value, 176-179
children owning and reducing
death tax, 119, 120, 180
college education savings and,
108-109
creditors and, 134
death tax and, 135, 180, 188
equalizing inheritances with,
188
first-to-die, 178-179
flexible, 178
income tax free, 91
level-premium term, 177
life insurance trusts and, 180
mortgage due dates and, 174
need for, 171-179
questions to ask first, 171-172
rating services, 179
second-to-die, 179
Social Security survivors
benefits and, 202
soundness of companies and,
65, 179
term, 176-177
trusts and reducing death tax,
180
universal, 178
variable, 178
viatical settlements and, 91
whole life, 178
Life insurance trust, 180
Life span
annuities for long, 63-68
effect on nest egg, 40-44
Life support. See Health power of
attorney; Living will
Limited partnerships
lack of liquidity with, 30

Lincoln, Abe, 87
Living trusts
avoiding probate and, 137-138
incapacity and, 92-94
joint tenancy compared to,
162-164
Living will, 92-94, 167-168
Loans. See also Mortgage
401(k) plan as source of, 49
Long-term care
government assistance and,
149, 153-156
preserving assets and, 149-156
Long-term care insurance, 149-156
Alzheimer's and, 152
benefits and, 152-153
day-care and, 152-153
disability insurance and, 184
financial stability of insurers
and, 153
inflation and, 152
Robert Wood Johnson
Foundation nursing home
insurance and, 155-156
level of needed care and, 152
Parkinson's disease and, 152
pre-existing conditions and,
152
Lost assets, 197-198
Web site, 197, 198
Lump-sum distributions from
retirement plans, 134
income tax on inheritance of,
165

M

Marital agreement, 125
beneficiary designations and,
124
joint tenancy and, 162-164
marriage and liabilities with,
159-160
moving and validity of, 141,
143

Marital agreement (continued)
  nursing home costs liability
    for and, 159-160
  QTIP trust, 124, 128-129
  qualified terminable interest
    trust, 124, 128-129
  remarriage and, 125, 159-160
Marriage (and Remarriage)
  beneficiary designations and,
    128-129, 181-182
  college aid and, 126
  death taxes and, 123, 166
  divorce and, 123-124, 127
  life insurance for spouse in,
    171, 179-182
  joint tenancy and, 123, 162-
    164
  moving and, 141-145
  nursing home care expenses
    and, 127, 159-160
  providing for spouse and,
    123-124
  QTIP trust, 124, 128-129
  qualified terminable interest
    trust, 124 128-129
  real estate and, 73-74
  second-to-die life insurance
    and, 179
  Social Security benefits and,
    127
  title to assets and, 123-124
  trust and, 123-124, 128-129
  will and, 123-124, 128-129
Medical, 159-160, 161
Medical costs
  effect on inheritances, 34, 35,
    42
  gifts and, 111
  marriage and liability for, 159-
    160
  MSA, 76
  nursing home costs and
    marriage's effect on, 159-
    160

parents and medical costs
    while traveling under, 161
  remarriage and liability for,
    159-160
Medical Savings Account, 76
Medicare, 149
  parents and medical costs
    while traveling under, 161
Medigap insurance, 151
Mistakes
  beneficiary designation, 181-
    182
  business, 187-189
  correcting, 59
  cost of, 47
  family business, 187-189
  joint tenancy, 162-164
  partnership, 189
  retirement investment, 47
  Social Security, 14
Mortgage
  credit report and, 96
  dangers, 22, 49-50
  deducting interest and, 22
  due dates, 174
  early payoff of, 69-72
  15-year loan, 69-72
  nursing home costs and, 150-
    151
  payment plans, 69-72
  prepayment penalties,
    avoiding, 72
  reducing interest paid on, 69-
    72
  reducing stress in, 72
  retirement years and, 49-50
  reverse, 150-151
Moving, 141-146
  health insurance and, 145
  income tax and, 144
  long-term care insurance and,
    149-156
  marital agreement and, 143
  nursing home costs and, 141-
    142

Moving (continued)
nursing home insurance and,
152, 155-156
property tax and, 144
purchasing residence and, 146
trusts and, 144
wills and, 144
MSA, 76
Municipal bonds
reducing income tax, 56-57
Mutual funds, 10, 28
college education saving
technique, 104
compared to annuities, 59
diversify, 47
life insurance and, 178
safety, 52
saving income tax and, 9-10,
28-29
variable annuities and, 67-68

N

National Association of Financial
Aid Administrators, 110
Web site, 110
National Association of
Unclaimed Property
Administrators, 197
Web site, 197
National Center for Retirement
Benefits, Inc., 16
Natural death declaration. See
Living will
Nest egg
annuities compared to, 63-64
assumptions in calculating, 39-
45
calculating college education,
112-115
calculating retirement, 39-45
size of, 34-45
when to start building, 34-35
New retirement math, 39

New York, long-term care
insurance in, 155-156
Nomination of conservator, 92-94
Normal retirement age. See
Retirement age
Nursing home expenses
California and, 155-156
Connecticut and, 155-156
Indiana and, 155-156
insurance and, 149-156
long-term care insurance and,
149-156
marriage and, 159-160
Medigap insurance and, 151
mortgage, 150-151
moving and, 141-143
New York and, 155-156
preserving assets and, 149-156
protecting assets and, 127, 149-
156
QTIP trust and, 124, 128-129
Qualified terminable interest
trust and, 124, 128-129
remarriage and, 127, 159-160
residence and paying for, 155-
156
reverse mortgage and, 150-151
Nursing home insurance. See
Long-term care insurance

P

Parents
beneficiary designations and,
181-182
business and, 187-189
death taxes and, 180, 187-189
family business and, 187-189
funeral arrangements and,
168
health power of attorney and,
92-94
homeschooling and, 87-89
housing and, 84-85

Parents (continued)
  income tax on inheritance
    from, 165
  joint tenancy and, 162-164
  living will and, 92-94
  marriage and medical costs
    for, 159-160
  moving considerations and,
    143-146
  nursing home costs and, 143,
    149
  part-time work and Social
    Security benefits, 86-89
  QTIP trust, 124, 128-129
  qualified terminable interest
    trust, 124, 128-129
  remarriage and medical costs
    for, 159-160
  remarrying, 123-125
  second-to-die life insurance
    and, 179
  selling residence and, 73-74,
    193-194
  Social Security benefits, 86-89
  stay-at-home, 86-89
A Parent's Guide to Wills & Trusts,
  206
Parkinson's disease. *See also*
  Incapacity
  long-term care insurance and,
    152
Partnership
  agreement on, 189
  death of partner in, 189
  disability of partner in, 189
  family business and, 187-189
  life insurance and, 171
  limited, 30
  title in, 189
Part-time work
  Social Security benefits and,
    86-89
Pension Benefit Guaranty
  Corporation, 16
Pension plan. *See* Company

retirement plan
PGBC, 16
Piggy bank
  savings technique with, 19
Place to retire, 141-145
Post-marital agreement. *See*
  Marital agreement
Power of attorney
  health matters and, 92-94
  incapacity and, 92-94
  money matters and, 92-94
Pre-existing conditions
  long-term care insurance, 152
Pre-marital agreement. *See* Marital
  agreement
Pre-nuptial agreement. *See* Marital
  agreement
Prepayment penalties on real
  estate, 72, 133
Prioritizing
  expenditures, 21-22, 46
  goals, 21, 46, 51
Privacy, 95-96, 206
Privacy Rights Clearinghouse, 95
The Privacy Rights Handbook, 95,
  206
Private pension plan. *See*
  Company retirement plan
Private retirement plan. *See*
  Company retirement plan
Private university. *See* College
  education
Probate
  avoiding, 137-138, 145, 162-
    164, 181-182
  beneficiary designations and,
    181-182
  joint tenancy and, 162-164
  living trust and avoiding, 137
  retirement plan assets and,
    134
Property tax
  moving and, 144
Prudential American Securities,
  196

Public education. *See* College
  education
Purchasing residence, 146

Q

QTIP trust, 124, 128-129
Qualified terminable interest trust,
  124, 128-129
Quality of life
  accelerated death benefits and,
    91
  grandparents and, 84-85
  home offices and, 84-85, 87,
    89
  homeschooling and, 87-89
  life insurance and, 91
  privacy and, 95-96, 206
  recreational vehicles and, 82-
    83
  RVs and, 82-83
  sandwich generation, 84-85
  simplification and, 81-83
  stay-at-home parent and, 86-
    89
  values and, 79-80, 87-88
  viatical settlements and, 91
  volunteering and, 79-80, 90
  working in retirement and, 90
Quicken, 204
  Web site, 205

R

Rates of return
  credit card interest and, 21-22
  for bonds, historically, 40-41
  for stocks, historically, 19, 40
Real bonds, 41, 47
Real estate
  agreement with partner on,
    189
  borrowing against, 45, 133,
    146

death of partner owning, 189
death taxes and, 166
disability of partner owning,
  189
granny house, 84-85
home equity loan on, 22
home offices, 84-85, 87, 89
income tax, 56-60, 73-74
joint tenancy and, 162-164
nursing home costs, 149-151
recreational vehicles, 82-83
refinancing, 22, 133
residence and saving income
  tax, 58-60, 73-74, 193-194
RVs, 82-83
saving income tax and, 193-
  194
selling, 45, 58-60, 82, 193-194
Record-keeping, 193-197
mutual funds and saving
  income tax with, 195-196
residence and saving income
  tax, 60, 74, 193-194
simplification and, 81
stocks and saving income tax
  with, 60, 195-196
U.S. Savings Bonds interest
  and, 197
Recreational vehicles, 82-83
Refinancing, 22, 70, 133, 146
Remarriage. *See* Marriage
Request for Earnings and Benefit
  Estimate Statement, 12
Residence. *See* Real estate
Retirement age
  effect of different, 27, 40
  later, 27
  normal, 11, 43
Retirement income
  examples of savings, 19, 23-24
  examples of savings
    requirements, 36-38
  life insurance and, 172
  sources of, 11, 34-35, 53-55, 90

Retirement plans. *See also* Roth
    IRA
  bankruptcy and, 134
  beneficiary designations, 181-
    182
  death taxes and, 166
  defined benefit plans, 15, 16
  distributions, 9, 10, 16, 18, 29,
    50, 58, 181-182
  early withdrawals, 54-55, 61-
    62
  401(k) plan, 15, 20, 64
  income tax on inheritance
    and, 165, 182
  IRA rollovers and, 50, 54-55,
    58, 61-62
  limits on FDIC insurance, 52
  lump-sum distributions, 182
  marriage and, 125
  National Center for
    Retirement Benefits, Inc.,
    16
  reducing income tax, 9-10, 53-
    55, 56-60, 61-62
  remarriage and, 125, 182
  summary plan descriptions
    and, 16-18, 62
  withdrawals, 49-50, 53-55, 58,
    61-62, 182
Retirement saving
  examples of savings
    requirements, 19, 23-24,
    36-38
  401(k) plan and, 20
  piggy bank and, 19
  right amount of, 34-35, 36,
    39-45
  when to start saving, 20, 27,
    34-35
Reverse mortgages, 150-151
Risk
  assessing comfort level of, 27,
    46-47
  avoiding, 27

Rollover. *See also* Retirement
    plans
  consider avoiding, 58
  Roth IRA, 53-55
Roth IRA, 9, 10, 24-26, 29, 30, 49,
    53-55, 57, 68, 106, 107
RVAmerica, 83
  Web site, 83
RVs, 82-83
  Web site, 83

S

Safe deposit box
  funeral arrangements and, 168
Sandwich generation, 84-85
Saving
  by record keeping, 60, 193-197
  by reducing death tax, 116-
    120, 124, 128-129, 180
  by reducing debt expenses,
    21-22
  by reducing income tax, 9-10,
    53-55, 56-60, 73-74, 184,
    193-196
  by reducing mortgage interest,
    69-72
  examples of, 19, 23-24
  retirement, 27, 34-35, 36-45
Savings bond
  See U.S. Savings Bonds
Second income, 86-89
Second-to-die life insurance, 179
Selecting a financial advisor.
    See Financial advisor
Siblings
  avoiding probate for, 162-164
  business and, 187-189
  death taxes and, 166
  disinheritance and, 162-164
  family business and, 187-189
  income tax on inheritance
    and, 165
  inheritance and, 162-164
  joint tenancy and, 162-164

Siblings (continued)
trusts and, 162-164, 166, 187-189
wills and, 162-164, 166, 187-189
Simplification, 81-83
Single premium annuity. *See* Annuities
Smartmoney Web site, 205
Social Security
avoiding divorce and, 127
benefit examples of, 201-202
children's benefits under, 11-12, 201-202
correcting mistakes in benefits for, 14
disability benefits, 11-12, 86-88, 202
divorce and 127,
form for benefits and earnings under, 12
integration, 15, 16
life insurance needed and, 175
marriage and, 127
normal retirement age for, 11, 43
part-time work and, 86-88
remarriage and, 127
Request for Earnings and Benefit Estimate Statement, 12
retirement benefits and, 11-12, 86-88, 201
survivors benefits and, 11-12, 86-88, 202
telephone number to request benefits and earnings form, 12
variable annuities and, 59
Web site, 14, 205
widows and widowers and, 11-12
Software for retirement planning, 204-205
Standard and Poor's Guide, 196

Stay-at-home parent, 86-89
Step-children. *See* Children
Stepped-up basis and income tax, 10, 28, 58-59
Stocks
saving income tax on, 10, 53-55, 57-60, 195-196
Stress
reducing credit card interest and, 22
reducing mortgages and, 72
Summary plan description
items included in, 16-18, 62
Survivors benefits
life insurance need with, 175
part-time work and, 86-88
Social Security source as, 11-12, 202

T

Tax Act of 1997. *See* Taxpayer Relief Act of 1997
Tax advisor. *See* Accountant
Tax credits, 60
Tax deductions
home equity loans and, 22
non-deductible interest, 22
Tax-deferral
adjustable life insurance and, 178
annuities, 63-69
beneficiary designations and, 181-2
cash value life insurance and, 177-179
flexible life insurance and, 178
investments, 24-25
nest eggs and, 42
QTIP trust, 124, 128-129
Qualified terminable interest trust, 124, 128-129
retirement plans, 23-26, 56-58
universal life insurance and, 178

Tax-deferral (continued)
    variable life insurance and, 178
    whole life insurance and, 178
Taxes. *See* Death tax; Income tax
Tax-free income
    accelerated death benefits and, 91
    avoiding in tax-deferred retirement plans, 57
    disability insurance as, 183-184
    life insurance and, 91
    maximizing, 56-57, 182
    Medical Savings Accounts and, 76
    MSA and, 76
    municipal bonds and, 56-57
    mutual funds, reinvested dividends as, 196
    nest eggs and, 42
    real estate, 73-74, 193-194
    Roth IRA, 9-10, 24-26, 53-55, 57
    stocks, reinvested dividends as, 196
Taxpayer Relief Act of 1997, 9, 25, 30, 53-55, 57-58, 73, 102, 105, 106, 124, 193
Terminal illness
    funeral arrangements and, 168
    health power of attorney and, 92-94
    living will and, 92-94
    money power of attorney, 92-94
    power of attorney, 92-94
Term life insurance, 176-177
Trans Union, 96
Trusts
    beneficiaries and, 42
    beneficiary designations and, 181-182
    business and, 187-189
    college education saving and, 103
    death tax and, 166
    family business and, 187-189
    401(k) plan and, 51
    irrevocable, 180
    joint tenancy and, 123-124, 162-164
    life insurance, 180
    living trusts, 137, 162-163
    marriage and, 123-124, 159-160
    moving and, 144
    nursing home costs and, 159-160
    QTIP, 124, 128-129
    qualified terminable interest, 124, 128-129
    real estate and, 73-74
    remarriage and, 159-160
    Taxpayer Relief Act of 1997 and, 30, 73-74
    will and, 123-124
Tuition prepayment plans and college education, 108

U

UGMA, 102
Umbrella insurance, 136
Uniform Gifts to Minors Act. *See* UGMA
Uniform Transfers to Minors Act. *See* UTMA
Universal life insurance. *See* Life insurance
U.S. Department of Education, 109
U.S. Savings Bonds
    calculating value of, 101
    losing interest on, 197
    Real bonds, 47
    Series EE and college education savings, 101
    Web site, 101
UTMA, 102

V

Values, 79-96
Vanguard, 204,
   Web site, 53, 205
Variable annuity. *See* Annuities
Variable cash value life insurance
   and college education
   costs, 108
Variable life insurance. *See* Life
   insurance
Viatical settlement, 91
Vital records, locating, 198
Volunteering, 79, 90
   Web site, 79

W

Waiver
   marriage and, 125
   retirement benefits and, 125,
      128-129, 159
Web sites, 14, 53, 79, 83, 95,
   101, 110, 197, 198, 203, 204,
   205
Whole life insurance, 178-179
Will
   beneficiaries and, 42
   beneficiary designations and,
      181-182
   business and, 187-189
   death tax and, 166, 187-189
   ethical, 79-80
   family business and, 187-189
   401(k) plans and, 51
   funeral arrangements and, 168
   joint tenancy and, 123-124,
      162-164
   living trust as compared to,
      137
   living will, 92-94, 167-168
   marriage and, 123-124
   moving and, 144
   nursing home costs and, 159-
      160

probate and, 137
QTIP trust and, 124, 128-129
qualified terminable interest
   trust and, 124, 128-129
real estate and, 73-74
remarriage and, 159-160
Taxpayer Relief Act of 1997,
   30, 73-74
Women
   name changes and Social
      Security, 13
   Social Security benefits for, 13
Work
   leaving and returning, 62
Working retirement, 90

Z

Zero-coupon bonds and college
   education cost, 110

Order Form

(Photocopy this page)

<table>
<tr><td></td><td>Qty.</td><td>Total</td></tr>
<tr><td>**BABY BOOMER RETIREMENT: 65 Simple Ways to Protect Your Future (2nd edition) by Don Silver**
240 pages $14.95 plus 5¢ s/h = **$15 per book**</td><td>____</td><td>$_____</td></tr>
<tr><td>Sales tax for California residents $1.23 per book</td><td></td><td>$_____</td></tr>
<tr><td>**A PARENT'S GUIDE TO WILLS & TRUSTS (For Grandparents, Too) by Don Silver**

Los Angeles Times: "Excellent book. It is clear. It is concise. It is clever."
256 pages $11.95 plus 5¢ s/h = **$12 per book**</td><td>____</td><td>$_____</td></tr>
<tr><td>Sales tax for California residents 99¢ per book</td><td></td><td>$_____</td></tr>
<tr><td>**(FOR QUANTITY DISCOUNTS, CALL 1/800-888-4452)**   Total</td><td></td><td>$_____</td></tr>
</table>

PAYMENT PREFERENCE:
   By check, payable to Adams-Hall Publishing or
   By credit card: Visa ___   MasterCard ___
                 Discover ___   American Express ___

ACCOUNT NUMBER:_____ EXPIRATION DATE:_____

NAME ON CARD:_____
                 (PLEASE PRINT CLEARLY)

   SIGNATURE:_____

PLEASE PRINT:

NAME_____

MAILING ADDRESS _____

CITY/STATE/ZIP CODE_____

DAYTIME TELEPHONE_____

**Mail to: Adams-Hall Publishing, PO Box 491002, Dept. BBR2,
      Los Angeles, CA 90049 or call 1/800-888-4452**

Order Form

(Photocopy this page)

Qty. Total

**BABY BOOMER RETIREMENT: 65 Simple Ways to
Protect Your Future (2nd edition) by Don Silver**
240 pages $14.95 plus 5¢ s/h = **$15 per book**   ____ $_____

Sales tax for California residents $1.23 per book $_____

**A PARENT'S GUIDE TO WILLS & TRUSTS (For
Grandparents, Too) by Don Silver**

Los Angeles Times: "Excellent book. It is clear.
It is concise. It is clever."
256 pages $11.95 plus 5¢ s/h = **$12 per book**   ____ $_____

Sales tax for California residents 99¢ per book $_____

(FOR QUANTITY DISCOUNTS, CALL 1/800-888-4452)   Total $_____

PAYMENT PREFERENCE:
By check, payable to Adams-Hall Publishing or
By credit card: Visa ___   MasterCard ___
                  Discover ___   American Express ___

ACCOUNT NUMBER:_____   EXPIRATION DATE:_____

NAME ON CARD:_____
                  (PLEASE PRINT CLEARLY)

SIGNATURE:_____

PLEASE PRINT:

NAME_____

MAILING ADDRESS _____

CITY/STATE/ZIP CODE_____

DAYTIME TELEPHONE_____

**Mail to: Adams-Hall Publishing, PO Box 491002, Dept. BBR2,
Los Angeles, CA 90049 or call 1/800-888-4452**